Simple Computer Tips for Busy People

Finish your work early with these powerful, easy-to-remember computer tips for non-techies like you!

Joe Rejeski

yddad-evol-gnihtyna-od-nac-yeoj-dna-allebasi

ISBN: 1543147445
ISBN-13: 978-1543147445

Table of Contents

Is This You? (a.k.a. Who This Book Is For)

Are your work days long and stressful?

Are you a non-techie who would like to work less?

What would you do with your afternoon if you were able to finish most of your work by lunchtime?

Most people spend a LOT of time on their computers, frustrated at times, wishing there was a sledgehammer in reach to give their computer the Gallagher sledgehammer-watermelon treatment.

They are spending much more time than they need to do their work, probably an hour or two a day.

They don't know simple computer tips for busy people.

I can help you save a lot of time, but the people I will never be able to help are the people who don't have time to learn computer tips.

They're too busy.

They're too busy to learn ways to be less busy.

They're too busy, because they are doing things the long way rather than taking the time to learn the shortcuts.

These people will continue the daily struggle against the avalanche of work, thinking that that's the way it's supposed to be, even though they spend the day working on the greatest time-saving device ever.

I wish I could help them, but they need to realize that learning computer tips is an amazing investment of their time.

You're different.

We're going to have you stop working through your lunch break and get you out the door in time to have dinner with your family.

A client once said to me, "Joe, I know there are ways I could be doing more with this thing…I just don't know what."

Sound familiar?

There are zillions of computer tips on the Internet, and they are all out there for you to spend many, many hours trying to find what you need. And many of those tips are for advanced computer users or aren't relevant to most people, at least on a daily basis.

Essentially, this book is for regular people who have the unsettling feeling that they could be doing more with their computer to make their life easier, but they are not sure where to begin and have no time to review hundreds of computer tips on the Internet to find the ones that are useful.

After 20+ years of working with technology and all sorts of people, I decided to create a book of simple, powerful ways that non-techies like you can save time every day.

Every tip in this book requires zero technical expertise. Even for those tips that are more than a few steps, if you just follow the simple instructions, everything should go smoothly.

Writing a book on how to work less using your computer is a tall order.

I needed to make some assumptions about you, the potential reader of this book.

First, this book is NOT for geeks. It's for non-techies who perform their work on a computer and want to find easy, simple ways to use their computer to finish work early.

After reading this book, you will still be unqualified to hold a conversation at a Star Trek convention.

Also, this book does not provide every computer tip anyone will ever need to know, because then it would have to include a lot of tips that most people DON'T need to know to make sure everyone's unique needs are covered. And there are many, many lengthy books that attempt to do just that. (Are you really going to spend time reading a 500-page computer book?)

This book is your launching pad to learning those important tips that will get you doing more in less time.

If the following describes you, then purchase this book now to start finishing work early. If not, maybe *Simple Computer Tips for Busy People* makes a great, inexpensive gift for a family member, friend, or coworker. ;-)

- You wouldn't describe yourself as a geek or an expert on any aspect of technology, and when there is a problem with your computer, you usually call someone in the I.T. support department.

- You work with a PC (a Windows computer), not a Mac. All tips work on computers with Windows 7, 8, 8.1, and 10. Almost all should work with Windows XP and Windows Vista. If you're not sure which version of Windows you own, just click the Windows Start button, type **"winver"**, and then hit the Enter key. For earlier versions of Windows, you need to click the Start button, click **"Run..."**, type **"winver"**, and then hit the Enter key.

- You regularly work with one or more of the applications in the Microsoft Office Suite (Outlook, Word, Excel, PowerPoint) or G Suite, formerly "Google Apps" (Gmail, Docs, Sheets, Slides).

- You're not looking to become an expert (at least not now) on any particular application, but you do want to know a few simple, powerful ways to do more in less time.

- You like Piña Coladas. And getting caught in the rain.

O.k.

Maybe one of those isn't an absolute requirement.

Ready to get started?

Start Here

You're probably going to want to jump right in and skip all this nonsense at the beginning and get right to the tips.

However, you'll get much more out of this book if you take ten minutes and read the opening chapters.

Keep Going

To improve is to change; to be perfect is to change often.

— Winston Churchill

If time be of all things the most precious, wasting time must be the greatest prodigality.

— Benjamin Franklin

Let's learn a few simple computer tips so we can finish work early!

Every day, millions of people are battling back an avalanche of work. Maybe they've avoided taking the time to learn computer tips that will help them get more done in less time or maybe they just don't know where to start.

Why?

They don't have time.

Really!?!

They don't have time to learn how to save time???

They're spending more time unknowingly doing things the long way, maybe because learning computer tips is BOR-ING!

Do you know what's boring?

A lunch break at your desk that is about as long as a coffee break.

Leaving the office around the time your family is finishing dinner.

Starting the next day catching up on the work you didn't finish yesterday…even though you worked late.

I want you to stop working so much.

It's time to get a little lazy.

Get lazy by letting the computer do more of your work.

Computer tips will save the day.

Computer tips are not just for geeks.

Get that geek thing out of your mind.

Computer tips are for anyone who wants to work less.

Simply put, the more computer tips you know, the less you work.

You have a choice. Continue working a lot or spend some time getting to know the tips in this book.

Computers have the power to do amazing things, but you need to invest the time to learn how to let it do more of your work for you so you can have more free time to do the things you enjoy.

You're not losing time in big chunks. You lose time in small increments all day, every day.

Those small increments add up to hours a day.

Joe, most computer tips just seem like they won't save me a lot of time.

Individually, a computer tip probably won't save any more time than one trip to the gym will drop twenty pounds from your body.

But, when you start combining the computer tips in this book, you'll be saving a LOT of time.

An hour or two a day is possible.

I've assembled simple, powerful, and practical computer tips that when combined will make you a force to be reckoned with. These tips are not complicated, esoteric tips that may have practical value once or twice a year. You're not going to find a tip on how to overclock your processor or design cascading style sheets in HTML.

Instead, you will find simple, super-useful tips for non-techies...regular folks who work with computers every day but have little interest in how they work. Tips for people who are old, young, and anywhere in between.

This is a book of simple computer tips that you can (and should) use all day, every day.

Invest the time in learning a computer tip a day, and you'll soon experience the pleasantly unsettling feeling that you think you have more work to do, but you can't think of one more thing that needs to be done.

Exactly!

The more computer tips you know, the less you work.

Before long you'll be wondering what to do with the rest of your day.

I have a suggestion.

Get away from your computer (and mobile phone) for a few hours.

Enjoy!

I'm Too Old to Learn Computer Tips

No.

No, you're not.

The Biggest Obstacle to Learning Computer Tips

I'm guessing the biggest obstacle is you're busy and you probably suspect there's a faster way to do something, but it's going to take longer to figure that out than to get by right now with what you know.

Am I right?

I'm up against the same roadblock.

Sometimes, I find it a challenge just to recognize that there may be a faster way. Usually, the clue is if I'm doing something repetitious.

For example, I realized that many e-mails I would send to clients had the same information that I would type from scratch. One day, I decided to figure out a better way. Now, I have a number of signatures that contain many typical responses to e-mails.

I just *right-click* my Outlook signature and then choose the response that makes sense.

It's a relief not to have to type those e-mails.

Computers are great at managing repetitious work. If you find that you are doing the same tasks every day, you'll save a lot of time if you take the time to figure out a better way.

How to Use This Book

First, keep this book next to your computer, so you can refer to it throughout the week.

Second, feel free to read the chapters in order or jump around to whatever grabs you. Or close your eyes, pick a tip at random, and then give it shot. (Just be sure to open your eyes after choosing a tip.)

Third, trying to memorize a number of tips at once probably will work about as well as breathing water. (Adults hate memorizing.)

We learn by doing.

Think about how you learned to drive to work.

Did you sit at home and memorize something like "Drive ten blocks, and then make a right on Maple Street. Then, drive for about a mile and make a left on Orchard Place....."

Did you repeat those instructions over and over until you couldn't forget them?

Or, did you write down the directions (or use GPS), followed the directions once or twice, and then had the entire route memorized?

You learned by doing.

You're really good at learning by doing.

Here are two computer tips....

1. Double-click to select a word.

2. Triple-click to select a paragraph.

Right now, double-click a word in an e-mail, document, or website.

The word was selected.

Now, triple-click a word in a paragraph.

The paragraph was selected.

Try double- and triple-clicking words a few more times.

You now know two useful computer tips that you can use throughout the day!

If you try these tips a few more times right now, you will definitely remember them.

But, if you just read a tip without trying it, it is very unlikely you will ever remember it.

Try everything! Some tips you read won't sound that useful until you try them.

My advice is to set aside ten to fifteen minutes a day to try each of the tips in one chapter. Don't skip any. Some of the best tips I know I almost immediately dismissed, because they didn't seem that useful when I read them. Most chapters have no more than ten tips, so it won't take you long to give each one a shot.

If you can practice each of the tips in a chapter several times, all the better.

Then, throughout the day, try to find opportunities to work with the tips you just learned.

If you practice the tips immediately after reading them, you will be amazed at how many you remember.

And, even if you can't remember exactly how to perform a tip, you'll probably at least remember that the tip exists, so you can quickly look it up in this book.

Your memory is much better than you give yourself credit for.

The more tips you know, the less you'll work.

The power of these computer tips is not how they work individually, but in how you COMBINE them throughout the day.

I expect some people will overlook this chapter, flip through the book, try a couple of tips that look easy, and then become disappointed because they weren't able to complete a three-day project in ten minutes. Maybe they'll even post an online review that the book sucks and I'm a doofus.

They missed the point.

It's how you combine these simple tips that will help you save a lot of time.

For example, let's say you are searching for a recipe for chocolate chip cookies, but you are allergic to nuts.

So, you open your web browser and Google "chocolate chip cookie recipe". Then, you start clicking through the links and read through each recipe until you find a recipe without nuts.

You'll probably spend ten to fifteen minutes before finding what you need.

However, if you combined several tips in this book, you could find what you need in seconds instead of ten to fifteen minutes, because….

- Your web browser is already open, because you configured your computer to automatically start it when you login.

- Google is open, because you configured your web browser to automatically open a tab for Google when the web browser starts.

- You used the minus sign (−) in your search, so recipes with nuts were not displayed (e.g., "chocolate chip cookie" recipe −nuts)

Google	"chocolate chip cookie" recipe -nuts	🎤 🔍

- Then, after clicking a link for a recipe in the search results, you used "Find" (**Ctrl + F**) in the web browser to search for the word "nuts" just to make sure there were absolutely no references to nuts in the recipe.

Amazing!

You just saved yourself ten to fifteen minutes by combining a few simple tips from this book. And that's just for one task. Think about how much time you could save every day by combining more of the computer tips in this book!

I Need Your Feedback!

A lot of work went into writing a book on helping you work less. I hope you find the advice in this book incredibly helpful.

If you have any feedback, positive or negative, I want to hear from you.

My e-mail address is below.

Did you read a tip that you love? Let me know.

Or, maybe you have a suggestion for a tip or chapter you'd like to see in a future edition of the book? I'm happy to consider your suggestions.

Also, all of the information in this book was verified, but sometimes things change. For example, maybe the URL to a website was changed, so the URL referenced in this book no longer works. If you notice an issue, please let me know.

Here's my e-mail address:

joe@SimpleComputerTipsforBusyPeople.com

Thanks!

About the Author

Did you hear the one about the stand-up comedian who started an I.T. support and consulting firm?

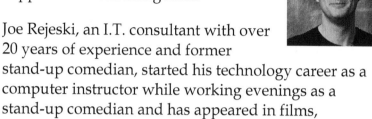

Joe Rejeski, an I.T. consultant with over 20 years of experience and former stand-up comedian, started his technology career as a computer instructor while working evenings as a stand-up comedian and has appeared in films, television, plays, and national commercials.

Over the years, Joe gained valuable experience working diverse I.T. jobs, and in 2004, he started the office I.T. support and consulting firm avenue X group with the core philosophy "simple is good".

Joe has helped thousands of people and built a reputation for explaining the complexities of technology in simple English.

Simple is good!

Connect on LinkedIn:

www.linkedin.com/in/joerejeski

Follow on Twitter:

https://twitter.com/JoeRejeski

10 General Computer Tips You Need to Know

Want to hear something funny?

Most people who use a computer every day don't consider themselves a "computer person".

People who work all day on a computer, and then often go home and spend more time on their computer, will decidedly declare that they are "not a computer person."

If you use a computer every day, you are a "computer person." (You're probably just not a geek.)

Me, too.

Geeks are fascinated by the way technology works. But you and I are fascinated by one very important aspect of technology — it saves us a LOT of time. (Oh, and it's fun...when it works.)

The trouble with non-geeks is we feel like outsiders and think learning about technology only has to do with understanding bits and bytes and *Star Trek's* "Kobayashi Maru," and we throw up our hands and declare, "I'm not a computer person!"

But, the more you know about the aspects of your computer that interest you, the more fun you'll have and you'll accomplish more in less time. Let's start with some easy things anyone can do, computer person.

Here are ten general computer tips you need to know. ALL of these are "Joe Favorite!" tips.

1. Many computer issues are resolved with a reboot. And the longer you go without a reboot, the more your computer will slow down until you restart your computer. Minimally, restart your computer once a week.

2. For better Google search results, be sure to use quotation marks around phrases.

3. When visiting a sketchy website, if you are prompted to install, run, or execute something, STOP. Whenever you install a program from a non-reputable source, it's likely there is a hidden virus in the program you are installing. Is watching that provocative video really worth taking the chance someone could indefinitely watch everything you're doing on your computer?

4. Your antivirus software should be configured to scan for viruses every day. Many people make the mistake of not configuring their antivirus software to automatically update and scan for viruses. Or, the antivirus license expired, so the software is no longer updating. Antivirus software without the latest updates is ineffective.

5. To immediately Save, use **Ctrl + S** as frequently as you type a paragraph. (You'll save much more frequently if you learn the keyboard combination than if you were to stick with using the mouse.) When a program crashes or your computer locks up, you will only lose the work that was created after the last time you saved.

6. Your backup system is the most important component of your computer. Every day many people lose years of work, because they didn't implement a backup, or if they have a backup system, they never checked to see if it was working. It is extremely important you understand this: BACKUP SYSTEMS JUST STOP WORKING AT SOME POINT. Don't wait until you've lost everything to test your backup system. If you don't know how to recover a file from your backup system, you should learn this asap.

7. To undo a mistake, press **Ctrl + Z**.

8. Before making any significant change to a document, spreadsheet, image, or any other file, take five seconds and make a copy of the file, so if you make a huge mistake you can easily return to the original file.

9. Use Task Manager to close programs that are frozen. You can access Task Manager by pressing **Ctrl + Shift + Escape** or by right-clicking your mouse in the taskbar (the bar at the bottom of your screen) and then selecting "Task Manager".

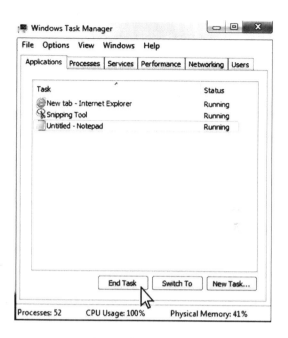

10. If it's been over a week or two, and you haven't learned a new computer tip, it's been too long. Flip through this book and try something new. Some of my favorite tips are those that I almost didn't try, because they didn't seem that effective at first read. Little tips and tricks add up to getting a lot more done in less time on your computer.

10 Awesome Things You Can Do with Google besides Performing a Search

Using Google to only search for websites? That's so '90s.

Release the Kraken with these ten gems.

1. Use Google as a calculator by just typing the numbers you would like to add, subtract, multiply or divide right in the Google search box (e.g., 0.09 * 456). And for you rocket scientists, you can even perform more sophisticated calculations such as square root (sqrt), sin, cos, and tan.

2. For tracking packages, you don't need to visit the shipping company's website. Just enter your tracking number directly in the Google search box to quickly find tracking information.

3. Use "define" to quickly lookup a word (e.g., define prodigality).

4. Have you ever spent days looking through a company's website for their customer service phone number? Why don't they list their contact information? Are they in the Witness Protection Program managing their website from a rumpus room in a suburb of Topeka? Just Google the company and "customer service" (e.g., "Verizon customer service").

5. Use "weather" to look up the weather in a city or zip code (weather Chicago). You can also look up "sunrise" and "sunset".

6. To get a stock quote, enter the ticker symbol into Google search.

7. Use "near me" to find just about anything near you (e.g., "guitar lessons near me").

8. You don't need to visit an airlines website to find arrival and departure times. Just search Google for the airline and flight number to find arrival and departure times for U.S. flights (e.g., jetblue 123).

9. For translating foreign languages, go to translate.google.com. You can translate text or even a website.

10. Use "set timer" to receive an alarm in a specified period of time. Make sure your speakers are not muted (e.g., "set timer 10 minutes and 30 seconds").

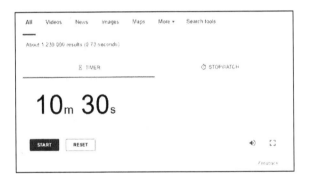

10 Google Search Tips

In a second you can perform a Google search...and a lifetime looking through the results.

Most people know how to perform a basic Google search, but then they waste time reviewing search results that don't have what they need.

We don't just want the results you are looking for somewhere on the first page. We want them at the top.

Use combinations of these simple search terms for quickly finding exactly what you need.

1. When entering a search term, consider what words may be on the websites you are searching for. When in doubt, just simply write exactly what you're looking for. Don't try to speak techie.

2. Case doesn't matter. Google doesn't care if words are uppercase or lowercase. However, one exception is the use of the "OR" operator.

3. Place quotes around phrases, so Google doesn't think you are searching for websites with the individual words (e.g., "moose and squirrel").

4. Use the minus sign to remove words from your search results (ex. "chocolate chip cookie" recipe −nuts).

5. Use "**OR**" (must be capitalized) when searching for websites that may use a different word or phrase than you expect (e.g., "red t-shirt" OR "blue t-shirt").

6. Use an asterisk (*) for words in a phrase you don't know (e.g., what does the * say).

7. Be sure to quickly refine your search by using the tabs **"All, News, Shopping, Images, Videos, More"** at the top of the search.

8. Click the "**Search Tools**" button to further refine your search. For example, let's say your search results show websites from years ago, but you prefer something more current. Select the dropdown "**More**", then select the dropdown "**Any time**", and then select "**Past month**" or "**Past year**". Or, you can select a "**Custom range…**" for a date range you specify.

9. Search for a range using ".." (e.g., Levi jeans $20..$30).

10. Google searches the entire Internet, but you can use Google to search a specific website, even if the website does not have its own search box. Just enter what you would like to search for followed by

"**site:*URL***" where *URL* is the URL of the website. This tip is not nearly as complicated as you may think. Give it a shot (e.g., paul newman site:tcm.com).

10 Web Browser Tips

We spend a lot of time on the Internet.

Sometimes we are working.

Sometimes we are checking out the latest "updates" to the Victoria's Secret website (I hear that even women visit this website, too).

Whether browsing cyberspace using Google Chrome, Microsoft Edge, Internet Explorer, or Mozilla Firefox, here are ten tips you need to know.

1. Have you ever been driven nuts by audio coming from somewhere unknown? If it's not your neighbor blaring Pat Boone's album *In a Metal Mood*, you've got another thing coming. Look at the tabs in your web browser. If a website is playing audio, you'll notice a speaker icon. You can mute the audio by right-clicking the tab and selecting **"Mute tab"**. (In Microsoft Edge, there are speakers on tabs with audio, but no mute button. Neither speakers nor a "mute tab" are available in Internet Explorer.)

2. You can reorder tabs by dragging them to different positions. Organize your tabs throughout the day in a logical order. I like placing the website I stream music from on the far left tab, so I can quickly mute the tab or listen to different music. Also, you can drag a tab away from the window to have the website appear in its own window as well as drag it back to rejoin the group.

3. Having a hard time viewing a website, e-mail, or document? Hold the Ctrl key while scrolling the mouse wheel to quickly zoom in or out. (The keyboard shortcut for zooming in or out is Ctrl and plus [+] or Ctrl and minus [−].) To return to the default view, click the **"Reset to default"** button that appears while zooming in or out.

4. You save files and folders on your desktop. Did you know you can drag links to your favorite websites to your desktop? Just hold down your left mouse button over the icon to the left of the URL in the address bar, and then drag the icon to your desktop. Whenever you'd like to visit the website, just double-click the icon on your desktop.

5. Recover a tab you accidentally closed by pressing **Ctrl + Shift + T** (definitely worth memorizing).

6. Would you like to jump back to a website you recently visited? Place the mouse pointer over the back arrow in the web browser, hold down your left mouse button (or right-click) to see a list of other

websites you recently visited. (Not available in Microsoft Edge.) For a more extensive list of websites you've visited, press Ctrl + H to review the History of websites you visited.

7. Interested in learning more about something you read on a website? Highlight a word or a phrase, right-click and select **"Search Google"**, **"Search with Bing"**, or whichever default search engine you have configured for your web browser.

8. Sometimes you're interested in clicking a link on a web page, but you don't want to move away from the web page you're currently visiting. Just *right-click* a tab and select **"Duplicate"** or **"Duplicate tab"**. For Mozilla Firefox, you need to hold the Ctrl key while clicking the reload button to the right of the address bar, but I might as well need to also rub my belly while wiggling my ears, because I'm never going to remember that, Mozilla.

9. Configure your web browser to automatically open websites you frequently access. Easy. Below are instructions for different web browsers.

Google Chrome

1. Click the three vertical dots in the upper-right corner of Google Chrome.

2. Click **"Settings"**.

3. In the **"On Startup"** section, select the radio button for **"Open a specific page or set of pages"**.

4. Click the **"Set pages"** link.

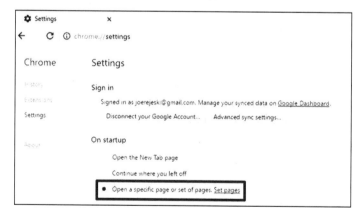

5. Add the URLs for websites you frequently visit, and remove the URLs for pages that you don't visit, and then click the **OK** button.

Microsoft Edge

1. Click the three horizontal dots in the upper-right corner.

2. Click **"Settings"**.

3. Under "Open with", select the radio button for **"A specific page or pages"**.

4. Click the drop-down arrow, and then select **"Custom"**.

SETTINGS	
Choose a theme	
Light	
Open with	
○ Start page	
○ New tab page	
○ Previous pages	
◉ A specific page or pages	
Custom	
about:start	×
http://google.com/	×

5. Add the URL for websites you frequently visit, and then click the **"+"** symbol to add the website.

Internet Explorer

1. Click the "**Tools**" menu. (If you don't see the menu, press the "Alt" key.)

2. Click **"Internet options"**.

3. At the top of the "**General**" tab under the "**Home page**" section, add the URLs for websites you frequently visit and remove the URLs for pages that you don't visit.

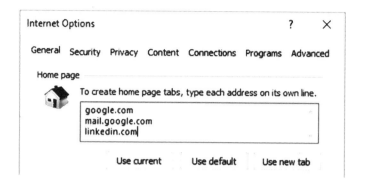

Internet Options   ?   ✕

General Security Privacy Content Connections Programs Advanced

Home page

To create home page tabs, type each address on its own line.

google.com
mail.google.com
linkedin.com

Use current   Use default   Use new tab

4. Click the **OK** button.

Mozilla Firefox

1. Open all the websites in separate tabs for all the websites you would like to automatically start when Mozilla Firefox starts. Be sure to close tabs with websites you do not want to automatically start when Mozilla Firefox starts.

2. Click the three horizontal lines in the upper-right corner.

3. Click **Options**.

4. Be sure "**General**" is selected on the left.

5. Click the "**Use Current Pages**" button.

10. Wouldn't it be great if you could simply click buttons on your web browser and be transported to each of your favorite websites as if you were changing channels on a remote control?

You can.

You can quickly and easily put links to your favorite websites underneath the address bar. Below are instructions for different web browsers.

Google Chrome

1. Go to your favorite website.

2. Show the bookmarks bar by clicking the three vertical dots in the upper-right corner of Google Chrome, and then select "**Bookmarks > Show bookmarks bar**".

3. Directly under the address bar, you should now see an area where you can add bookmarks.

4. To the left of every website's URL is a small icon. Just drag that icon down to the bookmarks bar.

If the name is too long just *right-click*, choose "**Edit...**", and then change the name to anything you like. Done!

Microsoft Edge

1. Go to one of your favorite websites.

2. Click the three horizontal dots in the upper-right corner.

3. Click "**Settings**".

4. Under "Favorites settings", click the "**View favorites settings**" button.

5. Make sure "**Show the favorites bar**" is set to "**On**".

6. Directly under the address bar, you should now see an area where you can add favorites.

7. Click the star directly to the right of the address bar.

8. Change the name to anything you like. I recommend shortening most names so you can fit more links on the Favorites Bar.

9. Click the drop-down arrow for "**Save in**", and then select "**Favorites Bar**".

10. Click the "**Save**" button. Done!

Internet Explorer

1. Go to one of your favorite websites.

2. From the **View** menu, select **Toolbars**, and then make sure "**Favorites bar**" is checked. (If you don't see the menu, press the "**Alt**" key.)

3. Directly under the address bar, you should now see an area where you can add favorites.

4. To the left of every website's URL is a small icon. Just drag that icon down to the Favorites bar. If the name is too long just *right-click*, choose "**Rename**", and then change the name to anything you like. Done!

Mozilla Firefox

1. Go to one of your favorite websites.

2. Show the bookmarks bar by clicking the menu icon (≡) in the top-right corner, and then select "**+Customize**".

3. On the bottom-left, click "**Show / Hide Toolbars**".

4. Make sure "**Bookmarks Toolbar**" is selected.

5. On the bottom-right, click "**Exit Customize**".

6. Directly under the address bar, you should now see an area where you can add bookmarks.

7. To the left of every website's URL is a small icon. Just drag that icon down to the bookmarks bar. If the name is too long just *right-click*, choose "**Properties**", and then change the name to anything you like. Done!

Power Tip: Entering Data in a Web Form

 Have you ever filled out a form on a web page, hit the **"Submit"** button, and then something happened that required you to type everything again (e.g., the web browser crashed)?

It happens from time to time, so to avoid retyping the text, whenever I need to enter a few sentences or more into a web form, before clicking the **"Submit"** button, I place my cursor in the area with the sentences, and then press…

Ctrl + A, and then **Ctrl + C**.

Why?

Ctrl + A selects all (everything). **Ctrl + C** copies the text.

If there is an issue and I need to complete the form again, I can just paste what I copied instead of retyping everything.

Power Tip: Jumping in a Drop-Down List

 Here's a quick tip.

When completing a form on a website, you don't need to scroll through all the entries in a drop-down list to find your selection.

Just press the first letter of the word you are looking for.

For example, to quickly find the state "New York" from a drop-down list of states, just click the drop-down list, and then press the "n" key to jump to all the states that start with "n".

10 Google Tricks That Have ZERO Work Value

Let's take a break and do a few things just for the fun of it.

What happens when you search Google for the terms below?

Well, you'll just have to find out.

1. Do a barrel roll

2. zerg rush

3. fun facts

4. Find chuck norris

5. Google in 1998

6. google.com/pacman

7. anagram (look at "Did you mean:")

8. askew

9. Enter an actor's name and then type "bacon number"

10. "flip a coin" or "roll a die" or "play dreidel"

10 Tips to Save Up to an Hour a Day with E-mail

Does your day start with you going through twenty or more new e-mails and then the rest of the day the hits just keep on comin'?

You probably think that this is just the way things are supposed to be with e-mail.

Battling back the avalanche of messages.

It's not.

This is the chapter where you will probably see the biggest immediate time savings.

It's also the chapter that requires you to invest the most amount of time.

It's worth it.

You're wasting a LOT more time with e-mail than you realize.

Don't just cherry-pick a few tips in this chapter.

If you're going to only pick a few tips that seem quick and easy, and ignore the rest, you're going to be disappointed.

Follow every tip in this chapter, and you can easily save up to an hour a day.

Don't have time to follow these recommendations? Isn't that exactly why you SHOULD be following these recommendations?

1. Consider Your Inbox to be a V.I.P. Room

The first thing we want to recognize is that your Inbox isn't a house party.

It's a V.I.P. room.

Only important e-mails are granted access.

Your focus is to prevent e-mails you don't need to read now from entering the V.I.P. room.

Your e-mail application has many features to help.

If e-mail is one of your most frequently used applications, doesn't it make sense for you to learn as many time-saving features as possible?

2. Unsubscribe, Unsubscribe, Unsubscribe!

Click the **"Unsubscribe"** link at the bottom of newsletters you never read.

That newsletter that you glance at every month and think someday you'll read, unsubscribe from that, too.

You can always subscribe again.

Since most newsletters are sent once a month, expect to invest the next month unsubscribing to newsletters. It's easy once you get in the habit.

You'll probably be surprised to learn how many newsletters are e-mailed to you every month.

If you really can't bear to unsubscribe from a newsletter or you don't want to offend someone you know by unsubscribing to their newsletter (they may see your name in a report of people who unsubscribed), refer to the section in this chapter on how to automatically move e-mails to folders. You can create a folder called "Newsletters" and automatically move newsletters from your Inbox to your "Newsletters" folder or even to your "Deleted Items" folder.

One caveat on unsubscribing: Avoid clicking the unsubscribe link on suspicious e-mails. It may open a website with malicious code, or you are confirming to a spammer that your e-mail address is active, which means they'll send you more spam.

The one newsletter you should never unsubscribe from?

Mine, of course!

3. Use the Delete Key

Your Inbox is not a junk drawer. Every item in your Inbox should have a compelling reason for being there.

Remember that time a year ago when Mary sent you an e-mail asking, "Do you have any paperclips?" and you responded "No"?

(BTW...I think we both know you actually had some paperclips.)

Why didn't you delete that e-mail?

Why are you saving e-mails that you will NEVER need to refer to?

Make friends with the Delete key. It's o.k.

At the end of the day, your Inbox should have no more than ten e-mails for the entire day. I like to try for five e-mails. Everything else is either deleted or filed away. Mainly deleted.

We all want to produce the e-mail out of thin air that vindicates us when wrongfully accused by some wrongful accuser! However, when you fill your Inbox with e-mails you'll never need to read again, it hinders you from being able to glance over those e-mails for the past few days that are important and may need a second look.

Every time you read an e-mail, ask yourself "Will I ever need to refer to this e-mail again?" and err on the side of "no."

4. Move E-mails to Folders

Some people think managing e-mail folders to be more work.

It's not.

Create folders for people or companies you regularly communicate with and move important e-mails to the relevant folders, and then delete the rest.

You'll be forced to ask yourself "Will I ever need this e-mail or should I just delete it?"

It's simple to create a folder.

And, save yourself a lot of work by having unimportant e-mails automatically moved to relevant

folders by using "Rules" (Outlook) or "Filters" (Gmail).

5. Automatically Move Unimportant E-mails to Folders

This might be the most important section of this chapter.

Remember, your goal should be to have only e-mails delivered to your Inbox that you actually need to read.

We want to minimize the amount of time you need to spend reading, moving, and deleting e-mails.

We're going to take advantage of **"Rules"** (Outlook) and **"Filters"** (Gmail).

You can easily create **"Rules"** or **"Filters"** to automatically move unimportant e-mails to specific folders so you can read them whenever you need to. Don't be intimidated. **"Rules"** and **"Filters"** are very simple and take only seconds to configure.

When Outlook or Gmail sees an e-mail from a particular sender, the e-mail will automatically be moved from your Inbox to a folder you specify. It's like your own personal assistant is automatically sorting your e-mails for you.

However, I recommend that you do not create **"Rules"** or **"Filters"** to automatically move important e-mails from your Inbox. Some people will create **Rules** to automatically move e-mails from a client to a folder named after the client's company. Then, they need to remember to review that folder for important e-mails. This approach works for some people, but remember the V.I.P. room? Your Inbox should be the central location for important unread e-mails. Once you read an e-mail, then move it to a folder, if you prefer.

Outlook

Here is an example of how to automatically move receipts from online stores from your Inbox to a "Receipts" folder in Outlook. Without the rule, every time a receipt is delivered it is one more unnecessary e-mail in your Inbox. Many people buy items from Amazon. Let's create an Outlook rule to move Amazon receipts to a folder called "Receipts".

You'll need an Amazon receipt in your Inbox. If you don't have an Amazon receipt, then find a receipt from any other online store.

1. Create a folder named "Receipts" by *right-clicking* your e-mail address at the top-left panel in Outlook, and then select "**New Folder...**".

2. Type "**Receipts**" and press Enter.

3. Go to your Inbox and locate a receipt from Amazon.com, but don't open it.

4. *Right-click* the e-mail, and then *left-click* **Rules > Always move messages from: Amazon.com.**

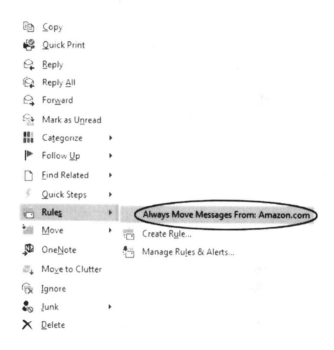

5. Choose the "**Receipts**" folder, and then click **OK**.

That's it!

Every Amazon receipt will be automatically moved to the "Receipts" folder.

In Outlook, you'll notice a number to the right of the folder indicating the number of unread e-mails in the folder.

If you ever want to quickly mark all the items as read in a folder, just *right-click* the folder and then click "**Mark All as Read**".

Gmail

Gmail uses "Filters" for automatically routing e-mails to "labels" ("labels" are similar to folders).

1. In Gmail, click the drop-down arrow in the bottom-right corner of the search box at the top of the window.

2. In the "From" field, enter the e-mail address of a sender for whom you would like to automatically move their e-mails (e.g., auto-confirm@amazon.com).

3. On the bottom-right, click "**Create filter with this search**".

4. Check the checkbox for "Skip the Inbox (Archive it)".

5. Check the checkbox for "**Apply the label:**".

6. Directly to the right, click the button for "**Choose label**", and then select "**New label…**".

7. Enter a name for the label (e.g., "**Receipts**"), and then click the "**Create**" button.

8. Click the "**Create filter**" button.

Unfortunately, Gmail does not display the number of unread messages next to the label, so you need to remember to check for new e-mails.

6. Think "Text Messaging"

You'll save yourself a lot of time if you avoid writing lengthy e-mails. Attention spans are not what they used to be. Most e-mails shouldn't be much longer than the length of a text message.

You may spend a half hour or longer crafting the perfectly worded e-mail, but after a few sentences, the reader is thinking about other things. Get to your point as quickly (and politely) as possible.

Also, avoid asking the recipient to answer more than two questions per e-mail, and whenever possible, try to make it one question per e-mail. The more questions you include in an e-mail, the more likely you'll need to follow up with e-mails to get answers to those questions that were overlooked or ignored.

7. Use the Phone

There are times when just making a two-minute phone call saves a lot of wasted time.

You can e-mail something like "Rosco, do you have time for a call now? I think we can address this matter much faster with a brief phone call rather than a number of back-and-forth e-mails."

8. Let Others Have the Last Word

Every e-mail does not require a response.

When you respond to an e-mail, often the recipient responds back, thereby creating another distracting e-mail for you to read...and respond to.

Sometimes no response is the best response, particularly when a number of people are included on an e-mail and they "Reply All" with valuable contributions like "Yay!!!"

Refuse to yay.

9. Use Signatures or Canned Responses

Computers should save us from performing repetitive work.

Most people use signatures for just their contact information, but your signature can also contain paragraphs of text. And you don't need to have just one signature. You can create multiple signatures with typical responses you often write.

In Outlook, if you create signatures with typical responses, you just *right-click* on your signature and choose the alternative signature with the relevant response to an e-mail you received.

In Gmail, you can create something called "Canned Responses", and then click the drop-down arrow at the bottom of a new e-mail to insert the relevant response.

You can create signatures and canned responses such as....

"FYI"

"Thank you for your interest in the position. We'll update you if you're a good match."

"Great meeting you! I'll send you the proposal shortly."

If you find yourself typing the same responses to e-mails, just take a minute to create a signature or canned response so you never have to type that text again.

Below are instructions for configuring signatures for Outlook and Gmail.

Outlook Signature Configuration

Time to complete: two minutes

1. Select **"File"**.

2. Select **"Options"**.

3. From the categories on the left, select **"Mail"**.

4. Select the **"Signatures"** button on the right.

5. To create a new signature, click the **"New"** button.

6. Enter a description for the signature that will help you remember the purpose of the signature (e.g., Meeting Request).

7. Click the **OK** button.

8. In the box at the bottom of the window, type all the text you would like to include in your signature (e.g., It was great meeting you. Are you available this week for a meeting or is next week better? - Samantha).

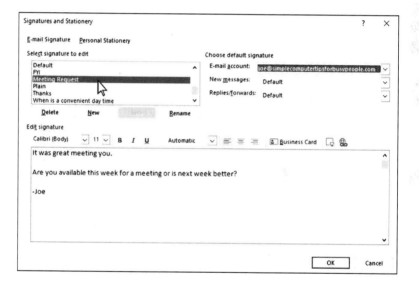

9. Click the **OK** button.

10. Click the **OK** button.

Create signatures for other typical responses to e-mails.

After creating a new e-mail, choose a signature by just *right-clicking* your default signature in the e-mail and a menu will appear listing all the signatures you created. *Left-click* the appropriate signature.

Gmail Canned Responses Configuration

Time to complete: two minutes

Before starting make sure that Canned Responses are enabled in Gmail by following these instructions....

1. In Gmail, click the gear icon in the upper-right corner.

2. Select **"Settings"**.

3. Select the **"Labs"** tab. (Near the top of the Gmail window towards the right.)

4. Select the **"Enable"** radio button for "Canned Responses".

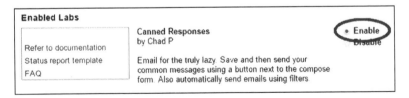

5. Click the **"Save Changes"** button.

To create Canned Responses....

1. Create a new e-mail containing the text you would like to include in e-mail responses. (e.g., It was great meeting you. Are you available this week for a meeting or is next week better? -Samantha).

2. In the bottom-right corner of the e-mail, click the drop-down arrow.

3. Select **"Canned Responses"**.

4. Select **"New Canned Response..."**.

5. Type a name for the canned response, and then click the **OK** button.

Create canned responses for other typical responses to e-mails.

After creating a new e-mail, choose a canned response by selecting the drop-down arrow in the bottom-right corner of the e-mail, selecting **"Canned Responses"**, and then choosing the appropriate response created by you.

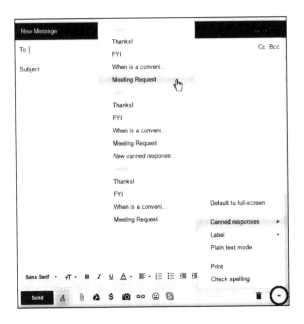

10. Don't Read Every E-mail as Soon as It Arrives

I'm not a fan of text messaging. (Yes, I'm the only one.)

I like the brevity, but text messaging implies, "Stop everything and give me your attention now!"

A similar expectation has occurred with e-mails. When a new e-mail arrives, we jump to read it. And then we respond to the e-mail or return to whatever task we were working on, so our attention is divided all day, every day. However, studies show that it's better to focus on one task until completion.

I read of one company that created a policy that required employees to disable e-mail notifications so the staff wouldn't be distracted every time a new e-mail arrived.

You'll get more done in less time if you take a similar approach.

Power Tip: How to Prevent Accidentally Sending Embarrassing E-mails!

Here is your (soon-to-be) favorite computer tip.

O.k.

You just sent your boss an e-mail describing all the wonderful things the two of you can do with some whip cream when you are alone together "in the parlor."

Maybe you attached some provocative pictures of your last rendezvous..."in the parlor."

Except, this e-mail wasn't intended for your boss.

Au contraire, mon frère!

The e-mail was intended for the love of your life whose e-mail address is similar to your boss's e-mail address.

CURSE YOU AND ALL YOUR HORRIBLENESS, AUTO-COMPLETE!!!

Wouldn't it be great to travel back in time and prevent this e-mail disaster from ever taking place?

If you are without a DeLorean and a flux capacitor, I'm going to show you another way to travel back in time and prevent an e-mail from ever being sent so you stay in a job, relationship, bowling league, etc.

In addition to being able to send e-mails, manage contacts, and schedule meetings, Outlook and Gmail have time-travel like capabilities that NOBODY uses.

Almost always we know right after hitting the Send button that we've mistakenly sent an e-mail to the wrong person.

But, it's too late.

Elvis has left the building.

However, few people know that you can (and really, really should) configure Outlook and Gmail to hold your sent e-mails for a short while, and then automatically send them.

The Outlook checkbox setting for "Send immediately when connected" has caused more embarrassment than the Selfie Stick.

We are going to uncheck the "Send immediately when connected" box and configure a delay, so you have just enough time to stop an e-mail from leaving your Outbox before you become known around the office as "Cool Whip."

With a delay it's almost like you can leap back in time to save yourself.

Also, in the event someone needs to receive an e-mail NOW, I'll show you how to immediately send an e-mail.

Below are the steps for configuring Outlook 2010, 2013, and 2016, but if you have an older version of Outlook, the steps are pretty similar.

Also, I've included the steps for configuring Gmail, but you better be pretty nimble, because Gmail does not give you much time.

Outlook Configuration

Time to complete: two minutes

1. Select "**File**".

2. Select "**Options**".

3. From the categories on the left, select "**Advanced**".

4. Look for the "**Send and receive**" section.

5. Uncheck "**Send immediately when connected**".

6. Curse the person who invented "Send immediately when connected".

7. Click the "**Send/Receive...**" button.

8. Under the section **Setting for group "All Accounts"**, be sure to check ALL five checkboxes.

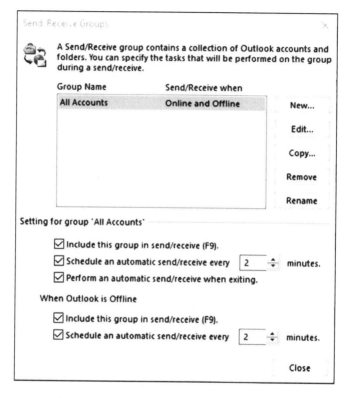

9. In BOTH sections for "**Schedule an automatic send/receive every**", be sure to change the setting to the delay you prefer. If you want to give yourself five minutes until an e-mail is sent, change the setting to 5 minutes. I would not set the delay for 1 minute in case the timing is a little off in Outlook.

10. Click the "**Edit...**" button.

11. Check the checkbox for "Include the selected account in this group".

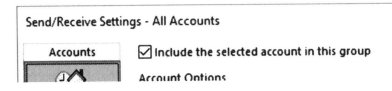

12. Click the "**OK**" button.

13. Click the "**Close**" button.

14. Click the "**OK**" button.

Done!

No more livin' la vida loca for you.

The next time you send an e-mail, keep an eye on your Outlook Outbox. The e-mail will stay in the Outbox for several minutes and then automatically proceed on course to its destination.

Want to stop the e-mail?

Open your Outbox, and then delete or open the e-mail.

WARNING! WARNING! DANGER WILL ROBINSON....

After opening an e-mail in your Outbox, you need to press the Send button if you would like to actually send the e-mail. If you just close the e-mail, it will remain in your Outbox, but it will not be sent.

And, if you have an e-mail you need to send immediately, pressing the Send/Receive button (the icon with two e-mails in the top-left corner of Outlook) will send all e-mails in your Outbox. The shortcut key for Send/Receive is **F9**.

Gmail Configuration

Time to complete: one minute

1. In Gmail, click the gear icon in the upper-right corner.

2. Select "**Settings**".

3. In the "**Undo Send:**" section, check the checkbox for "**Enable Undo Send**".

4. Set the "**Send Cancellation period:**" for as long as possible.

5. At the bottom of the page, click the "**Save Changes**" button.

When you send an e-mail, a box will appear at the top of Gmail.

There will be a link to **Undo**.

You don't have much time, so if you have any doubts, click the Undo link...pronto.

Power Tip: A Simple Secret for Getting Responses to Your E-mails!

 What do you think of e-mails you receive that begin with "Did you get my e-mail about…"

Hmmmm.

Now, you're put in the uncomfortable position of having to explain why you didn't respond AND answer the question from the original e-mail.

So, how do most people respond to the second e-mail?

Usually, the same way they responded to the first e-mail…they don't.

But, what if you're the sender? You want a response, right?

When you send an e-mail that starts with "Did you get my e-mail about…" you are making it unnecessarily hard on yourself to get a response.

Here's a technique I learned from executive coach, Larry Sharpe (www.TheNeoSage.com).

If you don't receive a response to an e-mail in a few days, send the same exact message again.

The same exact message.

What usually happens is the recipient will realize your original message was overlooked and will often be compelled to answer the e-mail the second time around.

The person who receives the e-mail the second time around doesn't need to answer your e-mail AND provide an excuse as to why he or she didn't answer your e-mail the first time. They are off the hook.

Does this technique guarantee a 100 percent response rate?

Of course not. But it will significantly increase your odds of receiving a response.

When most people resend an e-mail, they either retype the e-mail or go into their "Sent Items" folder and forward the message. If they're smart, they'll remove the "FW:" from the subject line to make the e-mail appear identical to the original e-mail.

There's a MUCH easier way to resend a message in Outlook. (Unfortunately, a similar feature is not available in Gmail.)

Here's a trick that I recommend that most people don't know....

1. In your **"Sent Items"** folder, open the e-mail that you would like to send again.

2. In the Ribbon at the top of the window, look for the **"Move"** section. You will see an **"Actions"** drop-down menu. Click the drop-down menu.

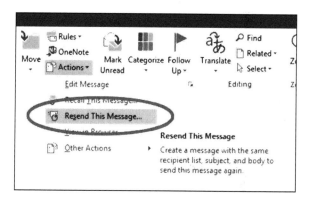

3. Click **"Resend this message..."**.

4. After reviewing the message, press the **"Send"** button.

You can even use this technique if you'd like to send the same e-mail to a different person. **Just change the e-mail address, and be careful that before sending the e-mail you remove any references in the e-mail to the first person to whom you sent the original e-mail.**

Power Tip: Getting Your Questions Answered

 If you've ever sent e-mails asking a few questions, you may have noticed that rarely are all your questions answered in the first response. Usually, you receive an answer to only the last question you asked in the e-mail you sent.

The only e-mail that will have all questions answered by the recipient is the e-mail that goes something like "Before I can send you your enormous check, please answer these 47 questions."

Guaranteed, all 47 questions will be answered.

In detail.

Whenever possible, limit your e-mails to one or two questions. If you have additional questions, I recommend following up after receiving a response to your initial questions.

Another tip is if you have questions you'd like a group of people to answer, do not send one e-mail to the entire group. The recipients will notice that others received the e-mail and, unless they have a strong need, most will likely not respond assuming others will respond instead.

If you need to send questions to a group of people, you'll receive a much better response if you send an e-mail to each person individually. You can save time by using the resend trick from the chapter "Power Tip: A Simple Secret for Getting Responses to Your E-mails!"

Power Tip: The Perils of E-mailing Word Files

It was like looking at a child standing on a scale that indicated 300 pounds.

It didn't make sense.

The Word document was only a few pages long and had a few pictures, but the file size was HUGE, far too big to be sent via e-mail.

A client had contacted me, because they were experiencing issues e-mailing a proposal in a Microsoft Word format to a prospective client.

Due to the file size, the proposal was repeatedly rejected by the prospect's e-mail system...thankfully!

As part of a troubleshooting effort, I enabled the revision history and lo and behold there before my eyes was every single change ever made to that document over the years. This was no ordinary document. This document was essentially a template the company used to create proposals for prospects.

Every pricing change.

Every revision of language.

References to other clients and prospects.

Many, many pictures that came and went.

They were all embedded in this gargantuan document.

It seemed that somehow "Track Changes" had been enabled (probably by mistake) on this document, thereby giving every recipient the potential to see all prior versions.

Imagine your prospects receiving a proposal from you allowing them to review the names and pricing of everyone else who had received a similar proposal from you.

Embarrassing.

Microsoft Word is a great application, and for many, a word processing standard. A similar issue can occur with other applications which is why when you are sending out documents, just turn them into a PDF.

Turning your documents into a PDF will lock it down and not retain the history of revisions.

Another reason to do the Word-to-PDF shuffle is your Word document on another computer may not show up as beautifully formatted as it appeared on your computer. Maybe the recipient doesn't have one of the fonts you used, so your document will be rendered with a replacement font that doesn't quite work. If your document is sent as a PDF, what you see is what they get.

When you're ready to convert your Word document to a PDF, just select **File > Save As**, and select **"PDF or XPS"**. Make sure "Save as type:" indicates "PDF".

If for some reason you have an earlier version of Microsoft Word or you are working with another word processing application that doesn't save files as PDFs, then try the free application CutePDF Writer.

http://www.cutepdf.com/Products/CutePDF/writer.asp

Since the application is free, please be aware of the subtle options to install other applications when you are installing CutePDF Writer.

CutePDF will create a printer called "CutePDF Writer". When you're ready to convert your file into a PDF, just print it to CutePDF Writer and the application will ask you where to save the PDF.

So, whether you're sending a proposal, a resume, or a love letter, create the document in your favorite word processor, but transform it into a PDF before sending it on its way.

Power Tip: E-mail Signatures on Mobile Phones

 "Sent from my iPhone" is great for Apple's brand but doesn't do much for you.

I recommend making your mobile phone signature identical to your Outlook or Gmail signature. (And, if you use webmail, make that signature identical, as well.)

Don't you want to be consistent and give the sense that you are at your desk working to help clients and prospects, even when you stepped away for a soup and a sandwich?

Also, I'm begging you...please remove "Sent from my mobile phone. Please excuse the typos." from your signature. Instead, type a little slower and use real words instead of abbreviations like "thx." Did you lose your ability to spell, because you are typing on a leprechaun-sized keyboard?

Well, top o' the mornin' to you, then!

iPhone

1. From the Home screen, tap "**Settings**".

2. Tap "**Mail, Contacts, Calendars**".

3. Tap "**Signature**" (you may need to scroll down).

4. Tap "**Sent from my iPhone**".

5. Type your signature so it matches your Outlook or Gmail signature.

Android Phone

1. Open the E-mail app.

2. Select "**More**".

3. Select "**Settings**".

4. Under "**Accounts**", tap your e-mail account.

5. Scroll down to "**Signature**" (make sure it is turned on).

6. Tap "**Edit signature**".

7. Type your signature so it matches your Outlook or Gmail signature.

8. Click "**Done**".

If you own another mobile phone model, just search online for something like this...

How to configure a default e-mail signature on a [INSERT YOUR MOBILE PHONE MODEL]

Power Tip: How to Use Your Computer to Send and Receive Text Messages

Do you do this....

You're answering e-mails on your computer when a text message is delivered to your mobile phone.

You pick up your phone and respond, and then back to your computer.

A little later, another text message arrives.

Pick up your phone.

Respond.

Back to the computer.

Why pick up your phone a dozen or more times a day?

Many wireless providers offer an app or a website that allows you to send and receive text messages from your computer. For example, Verizon has a website for text messaging (https://web.vma.vzw.com) as well as an app (Message+) that you can install on your computer.

If you send more than a few text messages a day, it's probably a good idea to have that app or website open all day on your computer while you work.

Just call your mobile phone provider and ask what they offer for sending and receiving text messages from your computer instead of your mobile phone.

Don't know their phone number?

Google "customer service" followed by your mobile phone provider.

If your wireless provider does not offer an application or website for sending and receiving text messages, there are other companies that offer this service.

Be careful if you're giving access to your private information to a company that is not your carrier.

Use E-mail to Send a Text Message

If you just want to send a quick text message using e-mail (e.g., Outlook, Gmail, etc.), just address your e-mail to the person's phone number (no dashes) followed by the domain of the carrier that the phone number belongs to. You can refer to the next page for a list of domains for popular carriers. (IMPORTANT: You need to know the recipient's mobile phone provider. If you don't know, just go to **www.carrierlookup.com**, and enter the recipient's phone number.)

For example, to send a text message to a Verizon customer with the phone number 123-456-7890, just address an e-mail to "1234567890@vtext.com". If the person is an AT&T customer and you sent the e-mail to "1234567890@vtext.com", the message would not be delivered. You would need to e-mail "1234567890@txt.att.net", instead.

If you save this information as a secondary e-mail address for contacts in Outlook or Gmail, you can easily recall this address when you need to send a text message using e-mail.

Remember, text messages need to be less than 160 characters, so keep that in mind when using e-mail to send a text message.

Here are a few addresses from popular carriers you can reference for sending text messages from your e-mail account.

- Alltel: *PhoneNumber*@**message.alltel.com** (text) or *PhoneNumber*@**mms.alltelwireless.com** (photos and video)

- AT&T: *PhoneNumber*@**txt.att.net** (text) or *PhoneNumber*@**mms.att.net** (photos and video)

- Boost Mobile: *PhoneNumber*@**myboostmobile.com**

- Cricket: *PhoneNumber*@**sms.mycricket.com** (text) or *PhoneNumber*@**mms.mycricket.com** (photos and video)

- Metro PCS: *PhoneNumber*@**mymetropcs.com**

- Sprint: *PhoneNumber*@**messaging.sprintpcs.com** (text) or *PhoneNumber*@**pm.sprint.com** (photos and video)

- SunCom: *PhoneNumber*@**tms.suncom.com**

- T-Mobile: *PhoneNumber*@**tmomail.net** (Be sure to include a "1" before the phone number.)

- U.S. Cellular: *PhoneNumber*@**email.uscc.net** (text) or *PhoneNumber*@**mms.uscc.net** (photos and video)

- Verizon: *PhoneNumber*@**vtext.com** (text) or *PhoneNumber*@**vzwpix.com** (photos and video)

- Virgin Mobile: *PhoneNumber*@**vmobl.com** (text) or *PhoneNumber*@**vmpix.com** (photos and video)

Power Tip: Send a Text Message to an E-mail Account

You can easily send (or forward) text messages to an e-mail account by simply entering the recipient's e-mail address instead of his or her mobile number in the text message.

10 Microsoft Office Tips

(Outlook, Word, Excel, and PowerPoint)

There are many great tips specific for each Microsoft Office application, but many of those tips have very specific purposes that are probably not relevant to most people reading this book.

As I started assembling the tips, it became apparent that a number of the same great tips apply to Outlook, Word, Excel, AND PowerPoint.

How cool is that?

Learn ten tips and apply them to four different applications!

These tips are the Swiss Army knives of computer tips.

1. Take the time to learn the keyboard shortcuts from the chapter "12 Keyboard Tips." Those shortcuts will help you get things done much faster in Microsoft Office.

2. Instead of adjusting the point size for a font, to quickly scale up or scale down, click the **"Increase Font Size"** and **"Decrease Font Size"** buttons. The

buttons are directly to the right of where you change the point size of a font. (The keyboard shortcuts are Ctrl +] and Ctrl +[, but those are two shortcuts I never remember.)

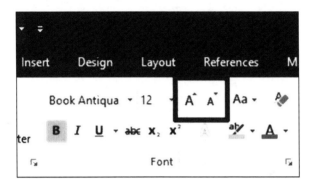

3. "Format Painter" will quickly change the look of text to match the look of other text in your file. Refer to the power tip "The Little Computer Tip That Could!"

4. If the look of some text is a mess, just select the text and then click the **"Clear All Formatting"** button or press Ctrl + Spacebar to remove all effects that change the look of the text.

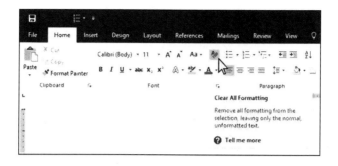

5. If you accidentally closed a file without saving, or experienced a power outage or application crash, there's a good chance you can recover your work.

   1. Save and close any open Microsoft Office files.

   2. Open the Microsoft Office application that is needed for the lost file. If you are prompted to recover the file, just follow the instructions.

   3. If you are not prompted to recover the file, go to **File > Info > Manage Document > Recover Unsaved Documents** ("Recover Unsaved Workbooks" in Excel and "Recover Unsaved Presentations" in PowerPoint).

4. Open the file you would like to recover, and then save it.

5. If you do not see your file, you can try searching your entire hard drive for ".asd" files. When searching, remember to include the period "." before "asd".

6. Many people lose time reading through lengthy documents or spreadsheets to find and resolve issues. Instead, use "Search and Replace". Not only can you search for text, but you can change fonts as well as search for extra hard returns (line breaks). And if you only want to perform a "Search and Replace" on a section of your document, just select

the area you would like to search before performing a "Search and Replace". It's a good idea to save a copy of your file before performing a "Search and Replace" in case something goes wrong.

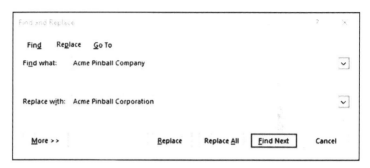

7. Configure Word, Excel, and PowerPoint to default to your favorite folders. **File > Options > Save** and change "Default local file location" to a folder you access the most.

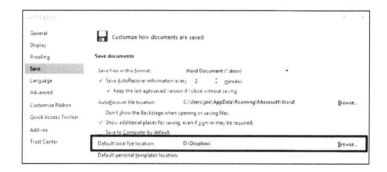

8. If you want the text you've copied to look like the text in the file you are pasting it into, don't just click the **Paste** button. If you click the **Paste** button, the look of the text will not change. Instead, click the drop-down arrow for the Paste button and select the icon for "Merge Formatting".

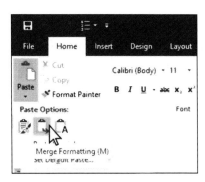

9. Here's an amazing Microsoft Office feature that I don't think many people know about. You can link data in different Word, Excel, and PowerPoint files, so changes made to one file are automatically updated in the other file. For example, I write proposals using Microsoft Word, but I create a spreadsheet in Excel that contains the financial information for the project. Then, I copy the spreadsheet in Excel, and instead of using "Paste", I use **"Paste Special"** when pasting the spreadsheet into Microsoft Word.

"**Paste Special**" prompts me to create a link to the Excel file. By using "Paste Special" to link the two files, I can make revisions to the spreadsheet that are automatically updated in the Microsoft Word file.

10. Sometimes when you press the Enter key, you'll notice that you move down two lines, instead of one. Press **Shift + Enter** to only move down one line.

Power Tip: The Little Computer Tip That Could!

This is one of my favorite computer tips that almost nobody knows about.

If you use any of the applications in the Microsoft Office Suite....you know I'm talking about you Outlook, Word, Excel, and you little imp, PowerPoint...then, you will want to get to know the little doodad known as Format Painter.

And, if you work with G Suite (Google Apps), there is a similar tool called "Paint Format".

So, what's the hoopla about?

Let me forewarn you that what I'm going to describe is going to first seem underwhelming until you try it a few times, so hang in there.

Essentially, Format Painter copies the look of some text to match whatever text you select. It's a beauty makeover for prose.

Are you absolutely kidding!?! That's it, Joe???

Wait...don't change the channel. I promise you'll love this one if you give it a shot. You probably have a need for this tip throughout the day, every day, and don't even realize it.

For example, let's say you copied text from a website or another document and pasted it into an e-mail. The text probably will not blend in and may even look all funky, like this....

𝔗𝔢𝔵𝔱 ℭ𝔬𝔭𝔦𝔢𝔡 𝔣𝔯𝔬𝔪 𝔜𝔢 𝔒𝔩𝔡𝔢 𝔚𝔢𝔟𝔰𝔦𝔱𝔢

If you would like that text to match the text that you are reading right now, most people select the text they would like to change and then play with the font, the size, the color, and the position until it looks right.

Too much work.

You can have this done in a second or two.

Instead....

1. Place your cursor anywhere in the text that looks the way you prefer.

2. Click **"Format Painter"** (Microsoft Office) or **"Paint Format"** (G Suite).

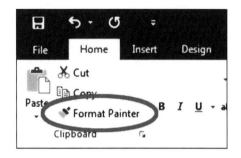

Ex. Microsoft Word

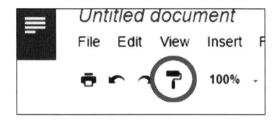

Ex. Google Docs

3. Select the text that you want to make pretty.

Done!

That's it!

And, here's a bonus...if you double-click **Format Painter** (Microsoft Office) or **Paint Format** (G Suite), it will remain active (until you click it again), so you can change the look of other text.

Format Painter can be used on text pasted from a website into Microsoft Word or an e-mail.

Excel users, Format Painter is great for changing the look of cells in spreadsheets. For example, if there are numbers in need of dollar signs, rounded to two decimal places and bold, just use Format Painter to match the look of a cell that already looks the way you prefer.

Try this tip now and you'll never forget it.

10 G Suite (Google Apps) Tips

There are many, many tools in the G Suite toolbox.

Here are ten tips to get you started.

1. Accidents happen. To help prevent sending an e-mail to the wrong person, make sure "Undo Send" is enabled in Gmail.

    1. Click the gear icon in the upper-right corner.

    2. Select "**Settings**".

    3. In the "**Undo Send:**" section, check the checkbox for "**Enable Undo Send**".

    4. Set the "**Send Cancellation period:**" for as long as possible.

Undo Send:	✔ Enable Undo Send Send cancellation period: 30 ▼ seconds

    5. At the bottom of the page, click the "**Save Changes**" button.

When you send an e-mail, a box will appear at the top of Gmail.

There will be a link to Undo.

2. If you keep a lot of tabs open in Google Chrome, use "Pin tab" to lock those important tabs on the left. Right-click a tab and then select **"Pin tab"**. The tab will move all the way to the left, and you'll also notice the "X" to close the tab disappears, preventing you from accidentally closing the tab.

3. G Suite will allow you to edit Microsoft Office files (Word, Excel, and PowerPoint) if you convert the files to a G Suite format (Docs, Sheet, or Slides). But what if you don't want to convert the files and prefer to maintain the files in their Microsoft Office format? To edit Microsoft Office documents in Google Apps, be sure to download and install the **"Office Editing for Docs, Sheets & Slides"** Google Chrome extension....

http://goo.gl/4rs8ts

4. Create documents by speaking into your microphone instead of typing.

1. Open a document in Google Docs.

2. From the menu at the top, select **Tools > Voice Typing...**

3. On the left of the screen, you should now see a microphone icon. Above the icon, there is a drop-down menu to change the language.

4. Click the microphone icon to start dictating your masterpiece.

5. Do you find yourself typing the same responses to e-mails? Use "Canned Responses" to create common replies to e-mails.

   1. To enable "Canned Responses" in Gmail, click the gear icon in the upper-right corner.

   2. Select "**Settings**".

   3. Select the "**Labs**" tab.

   4. Find "Canned Responses", and then select "**Enable**".

5. At the bottom of the page, click the **"Save Changes"** button.

6. To create a canned response, create a new e-mail with the text you would like to never have to type again.

7. In the bottom-right corner of the e-mail window, click the drop-down box.

8. Select **"Canned responses"**.

9. Select **"New canned response..."**.

10. Type a name that will help you remember what the canned response is about, and then click the **OK** button.

11. To use your canned response, just create a new e-mail, and in the bottom-right corner of the e-mail window, click the drop-down box and select the canned response.

6. Share files in Google Drive with anyone, including people who do not have Google accounts.

   1. Right-click the file.

   2. *Left-click* **"Share..."**.

   3. Enter the e-mail address of the person who should have access to the file.

4. Click the drop-down box to the right, and then select if the recipient should be able to edit, comment, or view the file.

5. Click the "**Send**" button.

7. Send e-mails with large attachments by just inserting Google drive files instead of creating attachments. You can send up to a 30 GB file by inserting a Google drive file.

1. Make sure the file you would like to e-mail is available on Google Drive.

2. Create a new e-mail. Include the recipient's e-mail address, subject, and a message.

3. At the bottom of the e-mail, click the Google Drive icon.

4. Select the file you would like to e-mail, and then click the **"Insert"** button.

5. Click the **"Send"** button.

6. Select **"Send without sharing"**.

8. What if there is an Internet outage or you're traveling with a laptop and need access to Gmail or your G Suite files? Configure offline access in advance, so you can continue working in Google Chrome until the Internet is restored.

Access Gmail Offline

You'll need to access the "Gmail Offline" app for accessing your Gmail when there is no Internet connection.

Here are the instructions for installing the app....

1. In Gmail, click the gear icon in the upper-right corner.

2. Select **"Settings"**.

3. Select the **"Offline"** tab at the top.

4. Click the **"Install Gmail Offline"** link.

5. Click the **"ADD TO CHROME"** button.

6. Click the **"Add app"** button. You now have the "Gmail Offline" app installed. You will need to access "Gmail Offline" when you are not connected to the Internet.

7. Click **"Gmail Offline"**.

8. Select **"Allow offline mail"**, and then press the **"Continue"** button.

9. Click the gear icon in the upper-right corner.

10. In the **"Download mail from past"** drop-down box, select your preference.

11. Click the **"Apply"** button in the upper-right corner.

12. Click the **"Close"** button.

When not connected to the Internet, you need to open Gmail Offline in Google Chrome by going to this URL....

chrome://apps

Unless you can remember that link, it's probably a good idea to bookmark that page.

Access Docs, Sheets, Slides, and Drawings Offline

1. In Google Drive, click the gear icon in the upper-right corner.

2. Select **"Settings"**.

3. Check **"Sync Google Docs, Sheets, Slides & Drawings files to this computer so that you can edit offline"**.

Offline	✓ Sync Google Docs, Sheets, Slides & Drawings files to this computer so that you can edit offline
	Not recommended on public or shared computers. Learn more

4. Click the **"Done"** button.

IMPORTANT: Before taking your laptop on the road, verify everything works properly by removing your network cable and disabling Wi-Fi.

9. You can directly access files in your Google Drive right from your computer by installing Google Drive on your PC.

   1. While connected to the Internet, go to Google Drive.

   2. In the upper-right corner, select the gear icon.

   3. Select **"Download Drive"**.

   4. Click the **"Download for PC"** button.

   5. Click the **"Accept and Install"** button.

6. You are prompted to save the installation file. Save the file to a folder on your computer.

7. In the lower-left corner of Google Chrome, you should see the downloaded file. To install Google Drive, click the file and follow the prompts.

8. Once installed, you should see a "Google Drive" icon on your desktop as well as a quick access link in File (Windows) Explorer. Done!

10. If you ever notice something isn't quite right with a file, maybe a lot of text disappeared for no apparent reason, you can review past versions of the file by accessing the "Revision History".

1. Open the file.

2. From the menu, select **"File > See revision history"**.

3. On the right side of the window, you will see dates and times for revisions made to the file. Just select the version you'd like to view. If you find an earlier version you'd like to make current, select the **"Restore this revision"** link.

Power Tip: Clipboard History

 You probably have a need for an application like "Ditto", but you won't know it until you start using it.

Ditto remembers everything you cut and copied since the last time you restarted your computer.

Have you ever copied and pasted a few items and then needed to paste the first item you copied, so you have to find what you need and select it again?

Ditto saves a history of text and images you cut and copy, so you can easily paste what you need, even if it isn't the last item you copied.

You can even copy a number of items from one file, one right after the other, then switch to another file, and then paste each item without having to switch back to the first file.

Amazing.

You can download it for free from....

http://ditto-cp.sourceforge.net

12 Keyboard Tips

You're probably going to want to skip this chapter.

Don't.

Keyboard shortcuts are essential for getting more done in less time, and I'm going to make it super-easy for you.

I know most people hate memorizing keyboard shortcuts, because there are so many confusing combinations to memorize.

I get it, BUT almost all of the shortcuts in this chapter have one easy-to-remember thing in common...the Ctrl (Control) key. The Ctrl key gives you control.

You can remember that, right?

Just like you hold down the Shift key when you want to capitalize a letter, you're going to hold down the Ctrl key AND another key to perform keyboard shortcut magic.

Now, it's going to get even easier.

The other key you need to press is often the first letter of what you're trying to do.

Want to Find something on a website or in a document.

Find?

Ctrl + F.

Easy.

Want to quickly Save a file or e-mail.

Save?

Ctrl + S.

Super easy.

Many will skip a chapter on keyboard shortcuts because of the fear their head will explode if they have to memorize something like a keyboard shortcut.

While it is a likelihood your head will indeed detonate before reaching the end of this chapter, should you be fortunate enough to escape this fate, you will be rewarded with some of the most powerful ways to do more in less time.

Joe, I can do things like "find" and "save" with the mouse. I'll just stick to what I know.

Before the invention of the mouse, we were forced to learn keyboard shortcuts.

The function keys at the top of your keyboard that no one touches anymore were the keys we needed to use to save files, spell-check, search for words, and any number of other tasks that can now be performed with a mouse.

With the mouse, there is no memorization required.

It's point and click.

But, it may not seem like it, the mouse slows you down.

Does taking your hands off the keyboard and moving the mouse to select one menu item take that much time?

No.

Does taking your hands off the keyboard and moving the mouse to select one menu item ALL DAY LONG, EVERY DAY take that much time?

Absolutely.

Experts agree that learning keyboard shortcuts allows you to work much faster in practically all applications.

When I started creating computer tip videos, I needed to learn about video editing.

I could have stumbled my way around only using the mouse to choose menu items, but I invested time in learning many keyboard shortcuts.

I'm glad I did.

It took little more time initially, but now I fly through editing videos.

And, when I search online for video-editing tips from the pros, almost everyone emphasizes that it's important to learn the keyboard shortcuts.

The best part about the keyboard shortcuts in this chapter is most will work in every single application you use!

Here are your top twelve keyboard tips.

1. Ctrl + S

Hate retyping work that you lost due to an application crashing, power outage, or some other mishap? Press **Ctrl + S** to save your work, and you'll have all your work saved up until the last time you pressed **Ctrl + S**.

"Save" starts with the letter "S", so this is an easy one to remember.

Joe, I'll just use the mouse to save.

Yep, I've heard that one.

There is absolutely no way you will save nearly as frequently when you use the mouse to save files.

Press **Ctrl + S** after you type a paragraph or two.

And, remember, you can press **Ctrl + S** when typing lengthy e-mails, so if something happens you can find what you saved in your Drafts folder.

Also, it's a good idea to never walk away from your computer without saving all open files. Who knows what will happen while you're away. And while you're at it, you might as well lock your screen. We'll get to how to do that in a minute.

2. Ctrl + P

The "P" in **Ctrl + P** stands for "Print".

Press **Ctrl + P** to print.

3. Ctrl + F

The "F" in **Ctrl + F** stands for "Find".

Search websites, files, Microsoft Word, Excel, and practically all other applications for text.

I frequently use **Ctrl + F** to quickly find text I'm looking for in a web page. You can take the time to read through a web page to find what you are looking for or press **Ctrl + F** and find it in a second.

For some reason **Ctrl + F** doesn't work in Outlook. The keyboard shortcut to search in Outlook is actually the F4 key…which I never remember, so for this one I just use the mouse to click the search box.

Let's take a quick break and applaud your efforts.

Was it that challenging to remember that **Ctrl + S** saves, **Ctrl + P** prints, and **Ctrl + F** finds? Doesn't the first letter of what you would like to do kind of give it away?

Is your brain screaming for mercy from all this impossible memorization?

Let's proceed on course.

4. Ctrl + A

The "A" in **Ctrl + A** stands for "All", as in "Select All".

Ctrl + A is awesome for quickly selecting All the files in a folder, All the text in an e-mail or a document, All the cells in Excel, etc.

5. Ctrl + Z (and Ctrl + Y)

"Z" is the last letter of the alphabet. Undo the last thing you did with **Ctrl + Z**.

Deleted an e-mail or file by mistake? **Ctrl + Z.**

Accidentally deleted some text? **Ctrl + Z.**

Spilled a cup of coffee on your pants. **Ctrl + Z.**

(Two out of three of the above will work.)

You can use **Ctrl + Y** to undo the undo. It's actually referred to as "Redo". If you press **Ctrl + Z** by mistake, just use **Ctrl + Y** to reverse the undo.

6. Ctrl + X, Ctrl + C, and Ctrl + V

Cut, copy, and paste.

You'll probably use these keyboard shortcuts the most.

The "X" stands for "Cut".

The "C" stands for "Copy".

The "V" stands for "Paste".

The three letters are located next to each other on the keyboard. If it helps you to remember, the "X" is like crossing/cutting something out. The "C" stands for "Copy". And the "V" is almost like a down arrow, as if it is pointing to the location to where you would like to paste the text.

If you paste something in the wrong location, no problem. **Ctrl + Z** to undo.

7. Ctrl + B and Ctrl + I

Bold and Italics.

Simple.

8. Ctrl + Home and Ctrl + End

Jump to the top or bottom of a website, document, e-mail, etc.

9. Windows Key + L

Stepping away from your computer? Let's lock it.

To Lock your screen, press **Windows Key + L**. (The **Windows Key** is that key on your keyboard with the Windows logo.)

You'll need to enter your password when you return, so make sure you know your password before locking your screen.

10. Shift + *Right Arrow*, Shift + *Left Arrow*

Select text using **Shift + *Right Arrow*** and **Shift + *Left Arrow***. This tip is handy when you missed the last character while selecting text using the mouse, so you don't need to select all the text again. (You could also hold down the Shift key and click with the mouse to select the additional text.)

11. Ctrl + *Right Arrow*, Ctrl + *Left Arrow*

I use this shortcut a lot.

Ctrl + *Right Arrow* and **Ctrl + *Left Arrow*** will move forward or back a word at a time.

12. Alt + F4

Immediately close a Window.

Useful if you hear someone sneaking up on you and you don't want them to see what you're doing.

Please be aware that if you attempt to quickly close a file that has not been saved, you will be prompted to save it.

10 Mouse Tips

The mouse revolutionized personal computing.

Wield the powers of this magnificent invention by downloading these tips to your brain!

1. Double-click to select a word. Triple-click to select a paragraph. **Ctrl +** *left mouse click* to select a sentence.

2. Have you ever missed the last character of some text you selected? No need to select everything again. Just hold down the Shift key and click just past the last character you would like to select. In fact, holding down the Shift key while pressing the right, left, up, or down arrows will also select (or deselect) text.

3. Hold the **Ctrl** key while scrolling the mouse wheel to zoom in or out.

4. To quickly move text, you don't need to select Cut and Paste from the menu. After selecting the text all you need to do is position the tip of the mouse arrow inside the selected text and then hold the left mouse button while you drag the text to a new location. Then, release the left mouse button. (If you drag using the right mouse button instead, you will be prompted to move or copy the text.)

5. Use **Ctrl** + *Left Mouse Click* or **Shift** + *Left Mouse Click* to select multiple items. For example, in File (Windows) Explorer you can select multiple files by clicking the first file (normal click without Shift or Ctrl), and then hold the Ctrl key while you click additional files. Or, to select a series of files, click the first file to select it, and then hold down the Shift key while clicking another file. Every file between the first and last files you selected will also be selected. **Shift** + *Left Mouse Click* and **Ctrl** + *Left Mouse Click* also work well for selecting cells in Microsoft Excel or Google Sheets.

6. In **Control Panel > Mouse**, go to the "Pointer Options" tab and select **"Automatically move pointer to the default button in a dialog box"**. Now, whenever you are prompted by a window to click a button, the mouse pointer will appear over the default button. Also, you may want to check **"Hide pointer while typing"** and **"Show location of pointer when I press the CTRL key"**.

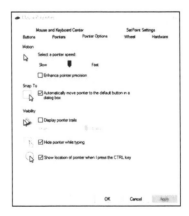

7. If you have buttons on the side of your mouse, customize them to go "forward" and "back". When web browsing, you can use these buttons to go forward or back a page. You should be able to configure these buttons under **Control Panel > Mouse**, or you may need to find the application on your computer that manages your mouse.

8. Double-click the title bar of a window to maximize it. (If the window is already maximized, it will return to its previous dimensions.)

9. Want to open a link on a website, but you don't want to lose the web page you are on? *Right-click* the link, and then select "**Open link in a new tab**". A faster method is to hold the **Ctrl** key while left clicking a link.

10. Clicking the right mouse button brings up a menu of commonly used options. For example, try selecting a word in an Outlook e-mail and then *right-clicking* the selected text. One of the options is to look up synonyms for the word. Or, try *right-clicking* a file or folder to see all the options that are available.

Power Tip: How I Configured My Mouse Buttons

Don't you think after purchasing his utility belt from The Home Depot, Batman configured it a little differently than the standard setup?

Many people are afraid of changing the default configuration of their applications and computer settings. Maybe they are concerned they might break the computer or mess everything up.

If you are working eight or more hours on a computer, I recommend you look for any way you can customize your settings to help you work faster. If you don't like the new settings, you can easily change them back to the original settings.

Configuring your mouse buttons is very simple and something worth doing. Typically, you make the changes in **Control Panel > Mouse**. However, if your mouse is made by a company such as Microsoft or Logitech, it's worth downloading from their websites a free application for doing more with your mouse. Just look at the bottom of your mouse for the model number, and then search either Google or the manufacturer's website for the application to download for that model (e.g., "Logitech m500 downloads").

Below is how I configured my mouse. Maybe you'll copy it. Maybe you'll do something different. But whatever you do, go crazy and make a change. Don't be afraid that you will mess something up! Remember, if you don't like it, you can easily return to the original settings. (Yes, even someone who knows very little about computers.)

My mouse is a standard mouse that also has buttons on the side. And the mouse wheel has an interesting feature. In addition to rolling the mouse wheel, it can be pressed to the left or right.

Joe's Mouse Button Configuration

Left mouse button = Default

Right mouse button = Default

Mouse Wheel (roll) = Scroll up or down (If your mouse wheel scrolls too quickly, you can modify the speed of the scrolling. Experiment.)

Mouse Wheel (push left) = Jump to the top of a document, web page, etc. (Same as **Ctrl + Home**)

Mouse Wheel (push right) = Jump to the bottom of a document, web page, etc. (Same as **Ctrl + End**)

Side button (front) = Advance a web page (or folder, if using File Explorer)

Side button (back) = Go back a web page (or folder, if using File Explorer)

10 Microsoft Windows Tips

Microsoft Windows is an operating system.

Let's put it another way.

It's the cookie jar that holds all the applications on your computer.

Here are ten tips that go great with a cold glass of milk.

1. Stepping away from your desk and don't want anyone seeing what you're really working on? To lock your computer just press **Windows Key + L**. (The *Windows Key* is the key on your keyboard with the Windows logo.) When you return to your desk, press **Ctrl + Alt + Delete** and enter your password (just like logging in). Obviously, don't lock your computer unless you know your password.

2. Is your desktop a mess of open windows? Use the mouse to click the "Show Desktop" button just to the right of the time and date in the bottom-right corner of your screen. If you prefer a keyboard shortcut, press the **Windows Key + D** (for Desktop).

3. You can rearrange open applications in an order that makes sense to you in the taskbar at the bottom of the screen. Just drag the applications to a new

location within the taskbar. (For example, I prefer Outlook to be in the far left for quick access.)

4. Use **Alt + Tab** to quickly switch to another open application.

5. Need to send a screenshot to someone? You can press the **PrtScn** key on your keyboard to take a snapshot, and then paste it into an e-mail or document. You won't see or hear anything happen when you press **PrtScn**. (It likes to maintain an air of mystery, I guess.) Actually, I prefer the "Snipping Tool", which is installed on all Windows computers starting with Windows 7. "Snipping Tool" allows you to select a portion of the screen.

6. Every now and then an application freezes...you see it on the screen, but it doesn't respond. To restart the application, you can restart your computer, or you can use Task Manager to close the frozen application and then open it. To start Task Manager, either press **Ctrl + Shift + Esc** or *right-click* the taskbar and select "**Task Manager**". To force an application to close just select the application, and then click the "**End Task**" button. However, if you force an application to close, you will lose any changes you made to an open file in the application that were made since you last saved the file. (You're saving frequently using **Ctrl + S**, right?)

7. To keep your computer secure and running smoothly, at least once a month check that the latest Microsoft Windows updates are installed. Before installing updates, be sure to close all open applications and make sure you have a current backup. You should restart your computer after applying Windows Updates. To check for the latest updates in Windows 10, go to **Start Menu > Settings > Update & Security > Windows Update**. For all other Windows versions, go to **Start Menu > Control Panel**. In the upper-right corner of the Control Panel window, change **"View by:"** to **"Small icons"**. Double-click the **"Windows Update"** icon. Click **"Check for updates"**.

8. *Right-click* applications in your taskbar (the bar at the bottom of your screen) to open a menu ("jumplist") to access websites or files you've recently opened.

9. Create your own customized menu of your favorite applications by pinning the applications to the Start Menu. For Windows 10, press the Start button, then *left-click* "**All Apps**". Find the application you would like to appear on the Start Menu, then *right-click* the application, and then *left-click* "**Pin to Start**". For other versions of Windows, press the Start button, and then *left-click* "**All Programs**". Find the application you would like to appear on the Start Menu, then *right-click* the application, and then *left-click* "**Pin to Start Menu**". Now, whenever you click the Windows Start button (the button in the lower-left corner of the screen with the Windows logo), you will see any applications you pinned. If you prefer, you can also pin applications to the Windows taskbar (the bar at the bottom of the screen).

10. Improve computer performance by disabling start-up applications you don't need.

   1. Press *Windows Key* + **R**.

   2. Type "**msconfig**", and then press the Enter key.

   3. Select the "**Startup**" tab.

4. Take a picture of your settings; so if there is an issue, you can return everything to the original settings.

5. Uncheck any applications that you do not need to start automatically.

6. Click the "**OK**" button when done.

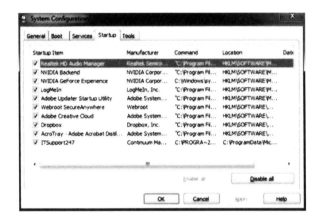

Power Tip: Magically, Delightfully, Automatically Start Your Favorite Applications!

 As you log in to your computer, magically, delightfully, automatically your favorite applications are summoned before your eyes as if you willed them to appear from the ether!

Outlook.

Google Chrome.

Microsoft Word.

iTunes.

All are at attention and steadfast in their determination to help you to take on the day!

Here is a cat's pajamas tip you can configure in a few minutes to automatically start your favorite applications whenever you log in.

When you start the day, you usually open the same applications on your computer.

Starting all of those applications can be…exhausting.

Let your computer lighten your load with this easy tip.

Essentially, all you need to do is copy shortcuts for your favorite applications to the Windows Startup folder.

That's it.

Follow these steps for automatically starting any application. You can even place in the Startup folder shortcuts to files you use every day.

1. Press the **Windows Key + R**.

2. Type "**shell:startup**", and then click the "**OK**" button.

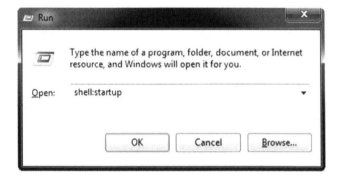

3. Copy any icon for an application or file to the Startup window that you would like to automatically start whenever you log in to Windows.

Done!

Here are some suggestions for applications to configure to automatically start ....

- Microsoft Office applications (Outlook, Word, Excel, etc.)

- E-mail applications (Outlook, Thunderbird, etc.)

- Web browsers (Google Chrome, Internet Explorer, Mozilla Firefox, etc.)

- Adobe applications (Adobe Acrobat, Photoshop, Illustrator, etc.)

- Quickbooks

- Skype

- iTunes

- Instant-messaging programs

Shazam!...all your favorite applications start every time you log in!

For your next trick....turning eight hours of work into four hours.

Power Tip: How to Quickly Clean Up a Messy Computer Desktop

 Is your desktop a junk drawer of computer icons?

If you have more than ten icons on your desktop, you probably are not clicking on most of them, so here's a way to clean up a desktop in a few minutes.

Relax.

Nothing will be deleted.

We all do it, but one of the worst places to save anything is on the desktop, particularly if you work in an office, because most offices do not back up desktop data. You're much better off saving your files to a network drive (assuming that your network administrator actually performs backups of the network drives rather than just saying he or she does).

Years ago, the wallet in my back pocket had so much stuff in it that when I sat down, it looked like I was sitting on a booster seat. It worked well at restaurants, because the hostess would bring me crayons and a placemat I could color on, but I yearned for menu options other than grilled cheese sandwiches and chicken nuggets.

Just kidding.

I love grilled cheese sandwiches and chicken nuggets.

Anyway, I was afraid to part with any of the items in the wallet.

What if I needed something one day and it wasn't there!

So, I tried something.

I removed everything from the wallet that wasn't essential. Items like driver license, a few important credit cards, and some business cards remained.

My wallet looked like it had gone through a Jillian Michaels makeover, and it felt good to sit down.

Reeeeaaal good.

I planned to see how long I could go without any of the other items.

I don't think one of those items I removed ever made it back.

We're going to do something similar with your desktop items.

We'll create a folder and move everything except a few icons you absolutely need into the folder. If you ever need one of those items, just open up the folder and drag it back to your desktop.

1. *Right-click* on your desktop, and then *left-click* **New > Folder**.

2. Give the folder a name (e.g., "**Junk Drawer**").

3. Open the folder.

4. Drag every icon you do not absolutely need into the folder, and then close the folder. To quickly select multiple items on your desktop, here are two tips....

   • To select multiple icons, hold the Ctrl key while clicking the icons.

   • You can quickly select a group of icons by holding down the left mouse button and dragging a box around the icons.

Done!

Power Tip: How to Restore the Windows Start Menu

 If you are using a later version of Windows and miss the classic Windows Start Menu, there are applications you can install that will return the familiar look of Windows.

My favorite is "Classic Shell", which you can download for free from….

www.ClassicShell.net

10 File Explorer Tips

(a.k.a. "10 Windows Explorer Tips")

You search, copy, open, and delete files.

Get un-busy with how you manage files.

1. To quickly start File Explorer (a.k.a. "Windows Explorer") press the *Windows Key* + **E**.

2. Want to Preview a file before you open it? Press **Alt + P** or from the **"View"** menu, select **"Preview Pane"**. Press **Alt + P** again if you want to disable the preview.

3. Click the column heading to sort by Name, Date Modified, Type, or Size. Click the same column heading again to reverse the sort order. You can use this tip to quickly find a recently created file by sorting by date.

4. Use **Ctrl** + *Left Click* or **Shift** + *Left Click* to select more than one file. Holding the **Ctrl** key while clicking each file name will select multiple files. Or, use **Shift** + *Left Click* by first selecting a file as you normally do (just click the mouse button without

holding the **Shift** key), and then **Shift +** *Left Click* to select another file to include all files in between the two files you selected.

5. Do you frequently access the same files or folders? Of course you do. Easily access them by adding them to "**Quick Access**" (a.k.a. "Favorites"). Just drag a file or folder to "Quick Access" on the left. Be careful, though. When you drag the folder to the "Quick Access" area, do not drop the folder on top of another folder or you will copy the folder. Instead, when you drag the folder over to the "Quick Access" area, release your mouse button when you see a black, horizontal bar. By using "Quick Access" you no longer need to browse through folders and subfolders to reach the folders you frequently access. Essentially, you are creating shortcuts to your favorite folders. Also, you can reorder the items by dragging them around. Place the most important items at the top or organize them alphabetically. And if you'd like to remove an item, *right-click* and select "**Unpin from Quick access**".

6. If you delete a file, immediately press **Ctrl + Z** to recover the file. (This command will work only with files in the Recycle Bin. If you bypassed the Recycle Bin by permanently deleting a file, Undo will not work.)

7. Be familiar with how to change the views and the size of the icons. On the "**View**" menu in the ribbon at the top of File Explorer, you can change the view to "**Extra large icons**" if looking for a picture and you want to avoid opening each image to find what you are looking for. And the "**Details**" view will show the file name, the date it was last modified, the type of file, and the size of the file.

8. Create a shortcut on your desktop to a file or folder by *right-clicking* the item and then selecting **Send to > Desktop (create shortcut)**. (You can also compress [a.k.a. "zip"] files and folders by *right-clicking* and selecting **Send to > Compressed (zipped) folder**.)

9. Use the Search box at the top of File Explorer to not only search for file names, but files that contain text you are looking for.

10. How does Google search zillions of websites and display the results in a fraction of a second? Indexing. Google doesn't wait for you to conduct a search and then start reviewing every website on the Internet. Google is constantly searching (crawling) websites and indexing keywords that appear on each website. Similarly, you should index the folders that you frequently access, so you are able to quickly find what you need whenever you perform a search in File Explorer. All you need to do is...

   1. Open Control Panel.

   2. Select **"Indexing Options"**.

   3. Click the "**Modify**" button.

   4. Browse to a folder you would like to index, and then check the checkbox next to the folder.

   5. Click the **"OK"** button, and then click the **"Close"** button.

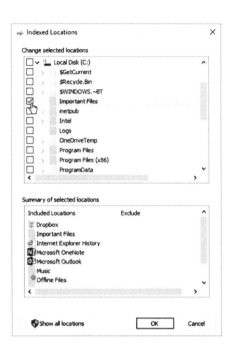

Everything in the folder and subfolders will be indexed.

You can index an entire hard drive, but I recommend you **do not index the entire C: drive or any of the "Windows" or "Program Files" folders**. There are a lot of Windows system files on the C: drive. Indexing your entire C: drive may result in performance issues. Instead, choose a folder on your C: drive that contains files you frequently access.

Power Tip: Back Up, Back Up, Back Up!

 There is no faster way to lose a lot of time than having to recreate years of data.

Back up your data today.

Right now, actually.

Viruses, hardware disasters, accidental deletion, fire, theft, etc. all can unexpectedly wipe out valuable data forever.

If you work in an office, do not trust that your I.T. department is backing up your data.

Seriously.

I've consulted with a number of offices where I was stunned to see the I.T. department or outsourced technical support firm had implemented an unreliable backup system and were ignoring issues that resulted in failed backups.

The company doesn't usually find out there is an issue with the backup system until something important needs to be recovered…but…is gone forever.

If it is not a violation of your company policy, buy a few USB drives and create a backup of your office data. I recommend sending an e-mail to your supervisor to let him or her know your intentions so no one thinks you are stealing company data.

If your home data isn't backed up, you have many options.

CrashPlan (CrashPlan.com) is one inexpensive service that will back up an unlimited amount of data to the Cloud (Internet). There is an individual plan for backing up one computer and a family plan for backing up two to ten computers.

Spend fifteen minutes getting a backup system in place.

And, do something that very few people do…practice recovering a file. If you practice recovering a file, you'll know how to quickly recover a file when necessary AND you'll be able to verify your backup system is working.

Do not assume that your backup is working.

10 Tips for Safe Internet-ing

You don't want to be the person the boss turns to and asks why you took down the entire company network.

In recent years, unethical people from around the world have discovered that they can make money, a LOT of money, by creating viruses that encrypt your data so you can't access it, essentially holding it hostage, and then offering you the key to access your data ONLY if you pay them a ransom. They can make a lot of money, particularly if the virus is unleashed on a company.

Companies are capable of paying much more money than most individuals can pay.

So, that's why we need to educate ourselves so we don't launch a virus on our computer and have to pay the bad guys to access our data.

There have been times I've told someone they have a virus on their computer and the person reacted like it's not a big deal.

It is a big deal.

The virus could be copying everything you do and sending it to a bad guy.

Here are some suggestions on safe Internet-ing....

1. Never write down passwords. Paper is lost or discovered by others. Either memorize your passwords or use a "password manager". (See the power tip "Use a Password Manager".)

2. Never e-mail passwords. When you send an e-mail, your e-mail passes through a number of servers. Someone could capture the text of your message and read it.

3. Make sure antivirus is installed on your computer and configured to automatically download the latest updates. Having an antivirus application installed on your computer is not enough. If your antivirus application is not routinely updated with the latest antivirus definitions, your computer is not protected. Two antivirus recommendations are BitDefender and Webroot, but remember, your safe Internet practices protect you much more than the best form of antivirus protection.

4. Call the sender of any suspicious e-mail attachments to verify the attachment was sent by them. Often, the bad guys will make it look like you are receiving an e-mail from someone you know. This is called "e-mail spoofing" and it is very easy to do. Just because you received an attachment from someone

you know it does NOT mean that the attachment was sent by them and it is safe to open.

5. Before opening any e-mail attachment it's a good idea to download the attachment to your computer, *right-click* the attachment, and then select the option to scan the file using your antivirus application.

6. Avoid risky websites, because malicious code (viruses) are often attached to risky websites. What's a risky website? If you need to look over your shoulder to make sure no one is around, it's a risky website.

7. Beware of "phishing" websites. Phishing websites are designed to look identical to the websites they are trying to emulate. For instance, to get your login information for your bank account, websites are designed to look just like the websites of popular banks. If you unwittingly attempt to log in to one of these phishing websites, you'll receive an error, but your login information is captured and the thieves will then attempt to log in to the real banking website and steal your money. To identify a phishing website, look directly to the left of the ".com" in the address bar. Let's use the banking website "chase.com". If you look directly to the left of ".com", it should indicate just "chase", and, yes, "chase" should be spelled correctly. It shouldn't be "cchase.com" or "chase123.com". Just "chase.com". Now, there may be legitimate subdomains at

"chase.com", such as "chaseonline.chase.com". Notice there is a period just before "chase.com". As long as the period is just before the domain name, you are probably safe. However, you may see a phishing website like "chase.abc123.com". I don't know if "abc123.com" is a legitimate website, but I know it's not a chase website, because directly to the left of the ".com" is not "chase". Always look at the text that precedes ".com".

8. Just because the link in an e-mail looks like it is for a legitimate website, it's possible that the actual link takes you to a different website with malicious code or a phishing website. In other words, the link you see in your e-mail is just for display purposes and can be anything. Someone can easily send you a link that appears to be for "www.Google.com", but when you click the link you are taken to a completely different website. The actual link is not immediately apparent, but in Outlook if you hover your mouse over the link in an e-mail and look carefully at the URL that appears, you can review the actual link to verify it is legitimate. If you're using a web browser to view e-mail, hover your mouse over the link and you will see the actual link in the bottom-left corner of the web-browser window.

9. If anyone calls you claiming to be from technical support, such as Microsoft or some other company, do not provide

access to your computer or tell them your password or provide any other information unless you are 100% certain that the person is someone authorized by your company to provide technical support. If you have the slightest doubt, get the person's name and phone number, and then tell them you will call them back. Then, check with your supervisor. Many hackers commonly sound authoritative when they call and will attempt to intimidate you into giving the information they need to access the network.

10. In addition to installing a reliable antivirus application on your computer, I suggest configuring OpenDNS. OpenDNS is a great service that identifies many websites with malicious code and helps you avoid them. You don't need to know this part to use OpenDNS, but essentially DNS translates domain names for websites into something that computers understand...IP addresses. It does this translation behind the scenes. You never see it. OpenDNS manages translating domain names to IP addresses and then blocks access to dangerous websites it has identified. Configuring OpenDNS on your router or computer is very simple. Below are the steps for configuring your computer. It may look like a lot of steps, but it's actually pretty easy. If you're in an office, check with your I.T. department before making any changes.

1. Open "Control Panel".

2. Open "Network and Sharing Center".

3. On the left, click **"Change adapter settings"**.

4. Look through the list and find the device that your computer uses to connect you to the Internet. If your computer connects using a network cable, look for something like **"Local Area Connection"**. If your computer uses Wi-Fi, look for something like **"Wi-Fi"**.

5. *Double-click* the device.

6. Click the "**Properties**" button.

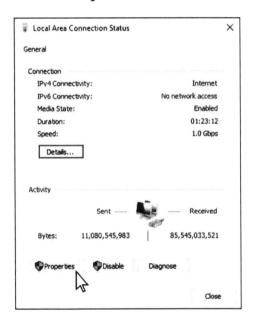

7. Select "**Internet Protocol Version 4 (TCP/IPv4)**", but do not uncheck it. (There is

an "Internet Protocol Version 6 (TCP/IPv4)", but it is very unlikely you are using that protocol.)

8. Click the "**Properties**" button.

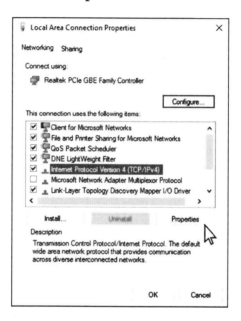

9. Take a picture or write down all the settings. (If there is an issue, you can then return to the original settings.)

10. Select the "**Use the following DNS server addresses:**" radio button.

11. For "Preferred DNS server", enter **208.67.222.222**.

12. For "Alternate DNS server", enter **208.67.220.220**.

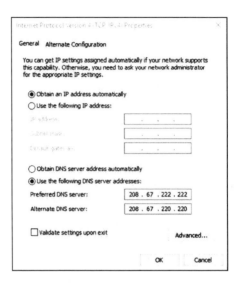

13. If you'd like to configure OpenDNS to also block adult websites identified by their service, use instead the IP addresses **208.67.222.123** for "Preferred DNS server" and **208.67.220.123** for "Alternate DNS server".

14. Save your changes and restart your computer.

15. Verify your settings by visiting the harmless test website "www.InternetBadGuys.com". You should see the message "This domain is blocked due to a phishing threat."

Power Tip: Use a Password Manager

 It seems every day you hear about a website being hacked.

If you use the same password for all of your website accounts, if one of those websites is hacked, then a hacker could attempt to log in as you by using the same password at other websites.

The solution is to have a unique, complex password for every website. But who can remember all of those passwords?

That's why you need a password manager.

A password manager seamlessly works with your web browser and can create a very complex and unique password for every website you visit.

Then, whenever you want to log in to a website, just click the shortcut in the password manager for the website and it will automatically log in with your unique username and password.

One of my favorite features is password managers can also remember things like your address, phone number, and e-mail address, so you can have the password manager automatically enter that information every time it's required for a website. For example, whenever you have something shipped to your home, have the password manager quickly enter your name, address, telephone number, and e-mail address.

A word of caution on using a password manager: Even if you are using a password manager, I recommend memorizing important passwords, such as banking passwords. You always want to be able to access your online banking at a moment's notice, particularly if for some reason an issue arises with your password manager.

Here are several popular password managers....

- 1Password (1Password.com)

- LastPass (LastPass.com)

- Dashlane (Dashlane.com)

- RoboForm (RoboForm.com)

Power Tip: Typing

Do you use both fingers when you type?

Is your typing speed one word per minute?

Maybe all that time you're not wasting by learning the basics of typing is actually costing you a LOT more time.

You have all day to improve your typing...or...all day to avoid improving your typing.

Learning how to type will help you finish your work faster.

Joe, learning how to type is BORING!

Typing.com has fun games that you can play where you can fight zombies, slice fruit (similar to "Fruit Ninja"), be a fighter ace extraordinaire, or spend the day at a carnival, all while learning how to type.

Why should kids have all the fun?

You don't need to learn all the keys at once.

Start off learning the home keys (a, s, d, f and j, k, l, ;), and then build from there.

www.Typing.com/student/games

Keyboard Ninja « Back to Games List

Ratatype

www.Ratatype.com

Ratatype offers a formal approach to learning how to type. From Ratatype's website....

If you increase your typing speed by 30% you can save 20 minutes daily. That's 1 year of your life saved in 20 years! That is why Ratatype is here. We want to save your life! At least part of it. So, Ratatype is a website for you to learn touch typing online. It is delightfully easy and completely free.

Power Tip: Too Busy or Too Distracted?

"Hey, Will, how's it going?"

"Busy! You?"

"Busy!"

These days it's almost required by law for conversations to begin this way.

Everyone is busy.

But, are we too busy or too distracted?

In our quest to work less, is the Internet friend or foe?

Shopping sites, chat applications, instant messaging, websites for our favorite sports teams, unmentionable websites, online games, videos on YouTube, pictures on Instagram, and Facebook. It's easy to lose an hour (or two) and not realize how much time you spent with online distractions.

For many years, none of these distractions existed in the workplace, so we needed to focus on one wacky thing...work.

We need to ask ourselves, is access to all these diversions helping us finish work early?

Probably not.

Do you have the courage to find out?

The application "RescueTime" (www.RescueTime.com) will monitor your computer activities and generate a report that lists how much time you are actually spending on different activities.

You'll even receive a "Productivity Score" on a scale of 0 to 100, so you can see if you are improving.

If there is one thing I'd change about RescueTime is your activity is transferred to RescueTime's website, so reports can be generated.

Their privacy policy
(**https://www.rescuetime.com/privacy**) indicates that
your information will not be shared without your
consent, you can delete your data at any time and they
do not "collect keystrokes, form input, screenshots, or
anything nefarious".

Also, you can pause RescueTime at any time.

RescueTime is a great idea and well-reviewed, but I'd
prefer it if I could just generate the reports without
RescueTime uploading information to their servers.

Another option is the application, "Freedom"
(www.Freedom.to). Freedom doesn't monitor your
performance, but it will block you from accessing
specific websites or the entire Internet for specified
periods of time.

Power Tip: A Cheap Way to Get More Done in Less Time

 Wouldn't it be great if you could buy something relatively inexpensive to get more done in less time?

Buy a second monitor.

I tell clients all the time that adding a second monitor is the cheapest, easiest way to get more done in less time.

Once exclusively used by financial wizards timing the stock feeds to know exactly when to buy or sell, second monitors are now on the desks of people in practically every industry.

But, until most people make the switch from one monitor to two, they don't know what they've been missing.

You spend eight to ten hours (or more) a day on a computer. You have a number of applications open all day; so why just have one monitor for all those applications to share?

There are probably many times you switch between applications to check on e-mail, refer to websites, or copy and paste text.

Sometimes you reference a web page while you are typing an e-mail.

Switching between applications is a lot more time-consuming than people realize and disrupts your workflow.

Some examples of things you can do with a second monitor....

- Keep e-mail open on one monitor while working on another monitor, so you don't miss an important new e-mail.

- Compare two documents, spreadsheets, websites, etc.

- Extend a large spreadsheet over both monitors.

- Copy and paste data between two files while viewing both at the same time.

- Work on one monitor while you wait for a task to complete (e.g., download a file, print, etc.) on another monitor.

- Remotely access another computer on one monitor while you work on your computer on the other monitor.

- Online chat with coworkers on one monitor while you collaborate on a project on the other monitor.

- Display a video on one monitor while working on another monitor.

A second monitor usually costs about $130, and if you think about all the time you'll save, it will pay for itself very quickly.

The one thing you will need to confirm is whether or not your computer has an available port (connection) for the second monitor and what type of connection it is. The most common types of connections are HDMI, DVI, DisplayPort, and VGA. (No need to understand what these terms mean.)

If you are unsure of the types of connections supported by your computer, just call the company that made your computer and they will help you verify if you can add a second monitor.

Also, you need to make sure that the monitor you are purchasing has the type of connection that is compatible with your computer. For example, if your computer only has an available DVI port, then you should purchase a monitor with a DVI port, as well. However, if your computer and monitor are not compatible, you can usually find an inexpensive adapter to make the connection.

1. Does your computer support a second monitor? If "yes", then....

2. What types of video connections does it support? HDMI, DVI, DisplayPort, or VGA?

3. Does the monitor you intend to buy match the video connection of your computer? (Most monitors support several types of video connections.)

If your computer does not have a port for a second monitor, you can add an inexpensive video card to your computer that provides the ability to connect multiple monitors, but you may need to enlist the assistance of a friend with a little technical know-how to assist with the purchase and installation.

Also, instead of two monitors, maybe you prefer just one big monitor. There are those who love a single large monitor on their desk, but that doesn't work as well for me. I prefer the separation of the two monitors so I can have an application open on each monitor, almost like I have two computers running at the same time. If I have only one large monitor, I would need to adjust the size of each window on my screen, so the windows are side by side. With two monitors, I just drag a window to each monitor and maximize.

Done.

DisplayFusion (www.DisplayFusion.com) is a great, inexpensive tool for working with multiple monitors. Unfortunately, some Windows versions don't place the taskbar at the bottom of both monitors, but with DisplayFusion you will have a taskbar at the bottom of all your monitors, plus a bunch of other great tools.

If you're not interested in DisplayFusion, a tip worth memorizing is that if you press *Windows Key* + **Shift** + *Left Arrow* or *Windows Key* + **Shift** + *Right Arrow*, the active window will move to another monitor.

And, that's it. You're all set to get more done in less time!

Power Tip: Trick for Restarting a Frozen Computer

If your computer has not responded for at least fifteen minutes, it's probably frozen and needs to be restarted.

To force your computer to power off, just hold the power button down for ten seconds until the computer shuts down.

Wait ten seconds, then power your computer back on.

Unfortunately, any work that was not saved will be lost, which is why one of my favorite tips is regularly saving by using the keyboard shortcut **Ctrl + S**.

(Stop only using the mouse to save!)

If you were working on something very important that wasn't saved and you really, really do not want to lose your work, then I would wait much longer than fifteen minutes to see if the computer un-freezes.

Power Tip: How to Make Your Computer Faster

Never in the history of computers has anyone ever said, "My computer is too fast. Somebody, anybody, please slow this thing down. It's working faster than I can possibly think!"

Below are some tips for improving your computer performance.

First, do not proceed with any of these tips unless you have a full backup of your computer and you verified that you are able to recover files from the backup.

If you don't have a backup, take a look at **www.CrashPlan.com**.

However, if your computer is more than five years old, it's unlikely you are going to see a significant change in performance. (Maybe it's time for an upgrade?)

Some people expect to jiggle the wires and suddenly a computer that was purchased seven years ago is going to start performing like a new computer.

With older computers there can be some performance improvement, but often it makes more sense to just buy a new computer.

You don't need to buy an expensive computer, but avoid cheap computers. Vendors are able to reduce the price of computers by installing trial versions of applications from other vendors. The hope is that once the trial is over, they will sell you the applications to make up for the low price of the computer. All those extra applications will slow down a computer.

Anyway, here are some suggestions on improving your computer's performance....

1. Thoroughly scan your computer for viruses to make sure there are no viruses causing performance issues. Use two applications to scan for viruses, but do not use both applications to scan for viruses at the same time. I recommend Malwarebytes and one other application (e.g., Webroot, Bitdefender, etc.)

2. At least once a month check that the latest Windows updates are installed. Before installing updates, be sure to close all open applications and make sure you have a current backup. To check for the latest updates in Windows 10, go to **Start Menu > Settings > Update & Security > Windows Update**. For all other Windows versions, go to **Start Menu > Control Panel**. In the upper-right corner of the Control Panel window, change "**View by:**" to "**Small icons**". *Double-click* the "**Windows Update**" icon. Click "**Check for updates**".

3. You may have some applications running that are slowing down your computer. Open Control Panel and select **"Programs and Features"**. Uninstall anything that looks suspicious or you don't need. If you are not sure what the application is for, look it up on the Internet to make sure you are not removing something important.

4. For some people the computer is not the issue nearly as much as the Internet speed. You should test your Internet speed and compare the results to make sure the speed is around the speed you pay your Internet Service Provider for. If the speed is accurate, then you may want to consider upgrading to a faster connection. Two popular websites for testing your Internet speed are....

www.SpeedTest.net

www.Speakeasy.net/speedtest

5. Download and install the free version of Ccleaner (http://www.piriform.com/ccleaner). Ccleaner has a number of tools for doing things like removing temporary files and web browser cookies, but make sure you have a reliable backup before using Ccleaner.

6. Disable unnecessary applications that automatically start.

   1. Press *Windows Key* + **R**.

2. Type **"msconfig"**, and then press the Enter key.

3. Select the **"Startup"** tab.

4. Take a picture of your settings, so if there is an issue you can return everything to the original settings.

5. Uncheck any application that you do not need to start automatically, and then click the **"OK"** button when done.

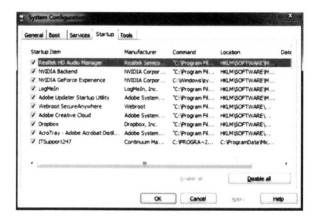

7. Add RAM (memory). Often, people confuse "memory" and "storage space". Storage space is actually the amount of space on your hard drive available for saved files. Unless you have very little space on your hard drive, making more storage space by deleting files or adding another hard drive will do little to improve the performance of your

computer. However, adding more RAM (memory) sometimes does wonders. And sometimes it does absolutely nothing. Unfortunately, you don't usually know if it will make an improvement until you add some RAM. RAM chips are thin, long chips that you add to your computer. Adding more RAM to a computer usually costs about $50 to $200 and is usually better left to a techie.

8. If the previously mentioned suggestions do not work, other than replacing the computer, the next best option is to erase everything on the computer and reinstall Microsoft Windows. Reinstalling Microsoft Windows is probably beyond the skills of most people reading this book, and that's o.k. If you plan on reinstalling Microsoft Windows, you should have two verified backups on separate media of all your data, in case something goes wrong with one of the backups (it happened to me once, and thankfully, there was a second backup). Don't forget to include files on your desktop or in other locations (such as e-mails) that may not be immediately apparent. Also, you will need all the drivers for your computer copied to a USB drive. "Drivers" are the programs that make things like printers, network cards, and video cards work. And you will need a copy of Microsoft Windows and the serial number as well as installation copies of all of your applications and their serial numbers. If you don't understand what you just read, you should ask for the assistance of someone who has installed Microsoft Windows several times.

Commencement!

Congrats!

You made it to the end!

I hope these tips help you get out the door early.

The more computer tips you know, the less you work.

Keep up with the latest time-saving simple tips by signing up for a brief monthly newsletter at....

www.SimpleComputerTipsforBusyPeople.com

Good luck!

—Joe

Do You Know an Office Looking for Amazing I.T. Support?

I started avenue X group in 2004 to provide offices the best I.T. support and consulting.

Our philosophy?

Simple is good!

avenue X group is based in New York City and Westchester, but thanks to remote access technology, we are very capable of supporting clients anywhere in the United States. We've regularly supported offices in New Jersey, California, Florida and Kansas.

To learn more about avenue X group and our way of saying thanks for referring us to a business, take a look at our referral program at....

www.avenueXgroup.com

Made in the USA
Middletown, DE
31 July 2018